The Coming Kingdom

WATERFORD
MENNONITE
CHURCH
GOSHEN, INDIANA

For no other foundation can any one lay than that which is laid, which is Jesus Christ.
—1 Corinthians 3:11

The Coming Kingdom
Don Blosser

The Brethren Press
Elgin, Illinois

Evangel Press
Nappanee, Indiana

Faith and Life Press
Newton, Kansas

Mennonite Publishing House
Scottdale, Pennsylvania

Scripture quotations, unless otherwise noted, are from the Revised Standard Version of the Bible, copyrighted 1946, 1952, © 1971, 1973.

A publication of The Foundation Series for Adults

Executive Director: Helmut Harder

Published by the Brethren in Christ Church, E. Morris Sider, editor; the Church of the Brethren, June A. Miller, editor; the General Conference Mennonite Church, Elizabeth Yoder, editor; and the Mennonite Church, Levi Miller, editor. Cooperative user: the Mennonite Brethren Church, Dennis Becker, editorial representative.

Designers: David Hiebert, Ken Stanley

The Coming Kingdom

Copyright © 1982 by The Brethren Press, Elgin, Illinois 60120; Evangel Press, Nappanee, Indiana 46550; Faith and Life Press, Newton, Kansas 67114; Mennonite Publishing House, Scottdale, Pennsylvania 15683.
Library of Congress Catalog Card Number: 81-66254
Printed in the United States of America

Contents

Foreword page 7
Introduction page 9

Unit A
Kingdom Theology

The idea of the kingdom of God is traced through Old and New Testament Scriptures, with the primary focus being Jesus' teachings about the kingdom.

1. The Hope of the Kingdom page 13
Jesus' teachings call persons to hope for and experience the presence of the kingdom in the midst of life and to anticipate the kingdom as fulfillment at the end of this age.

2. Love and Justice page 25
Jesus himself reveals the central message of the kingdom—that justice for all persons is the expression of God's love.

3. Signs of the Kingdom page 35
Through his ministry with people, Jesus provided signs of the presence and the coming of the kingdom—signs which were evidence of God's power available for all people.

4. Parables of the Kingdom page 46
Jesus' use of parables helps people to "see" and understand how God is at work in the midst of life and how people are involved in God's work.

5. Lord of the Kingdom page 57
The resurrection established the Lordship of Jesus Christ over people and over the forces of the world; the call to believers is to be faithful to the confession, "Jesus is Lord."

6. In the World But Not of the World   page 68
The Christian church and followers of Christ struggle with their relationship to the "world" and the tension of being "in the world" but not "of the world."

7. A People of Two Kingdoms   page 80
How are Christians to live in two kingdoms—with their calling to live life in the kingdom of God at the same time they are living in the kingdom of the world?

Unit B
Kingdom Living

Kingdom theology challenges Christians to address issues of poverty, hunger, and oppression in today's world, even as they live in anticipation of the future kingdom of God.

8. Entering the Kingdom   page 92
Jesus invites persons to respond in faith to his call to enter the kingdom, thus signalling their intention to walk in newness of life.

9. Affluence and Poverty   page 102
God's good creation is for all; the ethics of the kingdom calls for a stewardship of possessions so that all persons may share in the good of creation.

10. Plenty and Hunger   page 114
The biblical message is clear—kingdom living calls Christians to a daily concern for the issues of hunger and plenty in today's world.

11. Power and Oppression   page 126
Christians are to use their power for the good of others, proclaiming the message of a new way to a world in which power is often used to oppress others.

12. The Kingdom of Heaven and the Kingdom of Earth   page 137
What is the believer's relationship to political power—on the local, provincial, national, and world levels? And what does this say about the kingdom of God on earth?

13. Thy Kingdom Come   page 149
Christians participate in the present reality of the kingdom and also look with hope to the future when God's kingdom will be experienced in its completeness.

Bibliography   page 159

Foreword

From the earliest Old Testament days, the kingdom of God was a central theme in Hebraic life. In this kingdom, God was to be worshiped and served with heart, soul, mind, and strength. The Fall introduced a disruptive element which made the reality of the kingdom of God only partially available to humans. Then Jesus through his life and ministry proclaimed that "the kingdom of God is at hand," and invited believers to enter into participation in this kingdom which was in their midst here and now. Throughout the centuries followers of Jesus have recognized that, though they are living in the kingdom, the complete experience of living in unity with God—the coming of the kingdom in all its fullness—awaits a future promised day.

The Coming Kingdom explores this rich and intricate web of the understandings of kingdom theology and the experiences of kingdom living. Through an exploration of Old Testament Scriptures, Don Blosser introduces his readers to the vision and the hope that was central to Israel's life; though Israel at times lost the vision of God's future fulfillment, they were called back again and again to faithfulness. New Testament Scriptures reveal Jesus as the one who personified and expanded this vision of the kingdom, and present his followers confessing Jesus as Lord of the kingdom and inviting others to participate in kingdom life.

The author ably addresses an on-going tension which is closely related to the theme of the kingdom: how do persons affirm life in the kingdom of God and at the same time live in the kingdom of this world? This tension was present when Jesus and his disciples walked and talked in Galilee; it continued as the early apostles and the young church struggled to know what it meant to live as followers in an alien society; the struggle with this question was a major part of the early Anabaptists' life; and this tension remains a current issue for believers today. How do we live in the two kingdoms—the kingdom of this world and the kingdom of God?

Don Blosser's informative and challenging study looks at the kingdom of God through a careful study of biblical texts and from the perspective of the Anabaptist tradition. In the first unit, "Kingdom Theology," Old and New Testament texts are explored as the basis for a clearer understanding of the theology of the kingdom. This theology then becomes the basis for looking at the ethics of life in the kingdom and leads into the second unit, "Kingdom Living." What do Christians who are participating in the kingdom of God have to say to the hard issues of poverty and affluence, hunger and plenty, oppression and power, and the relationship of Christians to the state? How is our theology practiced in our life?

In *The Coming Kingdom,* Don Blosser has shared much richness of thought; this book will raise many thought-provoking questions, as well as offer challenging ideas for finding answers to the questions. Both for individual and for group study, this will be a valuable resource for helping persons discover more about life in the kingdom of God.

The Coming Kingdom is the fourth of eight studies in The Foundation Series for Adults. (For an outline of the two-year curriculum, see the inside back cover of this book.) Each of these studies, focusing on an aspect of the Christian faith which has been significant for the Anabaptists, is approached through careful examination of the Scriptures. The hope is that these studies of the Scriptures and the faith will help both individuals and congregational groups to experience renewal in their lives and new commitment to life in God's kingdom.—June A. Miller, editor.

Introduction

When we talk together, we use words. As we use certain words we have mental pictures that go along with the words, so that we "know" what we are talking about or at least what we mean by the words we use. In the mind of another person, however, the same words may create different pictures. Sometimes in a conversation we need to stop talking in order to look at the pictures (the definitions of the words) which we have in our minds. We see this most vividly when we try to communicate with someone who speaks a different native language. Then we have to explain what words mean in order to communicate effectively.

But this is also true when two persons speak the same language. In moving from one community to another, we may discover a different set of meanings for words within the same basic language. Normally, as we talk, we do not pay much attention to the pictures in our minds, until the conversation breaks down and misunderstandings occur.

A simple two-person conversation can be illustrated as follows:

'A' talks to 'B' and then 'B' answers 'A'. This pattern is repeated as two persons visit. What could possibly go wrong in such a simple interchange? The problem is simply that it isn't that simple! When A uses words, she has a picture or concept in her mind. When B uses words, he also has a picture or concept in his mind. When these pictures or concepts do not match, it is difficult to carry on the conversation.

For example: A and B are talking about a house. A has in mind an old, two-story, white frame building in the country. But when B uses the word "house," he means a red brick row house on a city street, with no front yard, only a sidewalk. Each definition (picture) is correct and valid, but unless both speakers can clarify their concept of "house," their communication is headed for trouble.

What does all this have to do with the kingdom of God? The phrase "kingdom of God" is one which often leads to confusion in conversation. Each person using the phrase has a general idea of what it means. Yet as we listen to conversations in church or religious broadcasting on radio or TV, it becomes clear that people have very different ideas about the kingdom of God—where it is, when it is, and how we get into it.

Although the words "kingdom of God" do not appear in the Old Testament, the idea of God's kingdom is found in the prophets. The prophets recognized God as Lord and king of all the earth (Psa. 47:2; 95:1-5). They also expressed hope for the day when God would rule over Israel in a special way (Isa. 24:23; 52:9-10). The prophets expected that God's rule would be realized in Israel's history; they anticipated a day when this rule would be fully experienced by all nations. A major theme in the Old Testament was this hope of the coming kingdom of God. God would bring this kingdom through the Messiah who would have many of the characteristics of King David. The Messiah would bring national liberation through military victories. In this way God would save his people (Isa. 35:4; Zech. 2:10-11).

This coming kingdom of God must have seemed far away in the century prior to Jesus' birth. This was a dismal period in Israel's history. Politically, the country and people were devastated. It was a time of wars, most of which

Israel lost; of guerrilla actions which kept alive the vision of freedom, but killed thousands of people; of hunger and starvation, caused by the demands for food made by the military and a few years of drought. All in all, it was a time of despair; it seemed as though God had turned his back on Israel.

Religiously, things were not much better. Israel remembered the days when God had spoken through the prophets. Granted, Israel had not always been kind to the prophets who proclaimed God's will, but at least they had known that God cared. Now, even the voice of God was silent, and the religious community was falling apart. The Essenes had withdrawn, going off into the hills to remain pure and separate from any contact with the traditional religious community. The Sadducees were trying to work out compromises that would allow the religious observances to continue without offending the Romans. The Pharisees' faith had become a set of clearly defined rules to be followed. The people were pleading for a voice from God. Even if they couldn't hear God's voice directly, they were hoping that at least God might speak to them through an echo bouncing off the temple walls!

Then one day a radical prophet appeared, calling the nation to repentance. People began to listen, to flock to hear him, to be baptized in the Jordan River, in the Sea of Galilee, anywhere, as they responded to the message of this unconventional prophet. People talked of the arrival of the Messiah, and once more hope was felt.

Then another voice was heard, speaking with authority and confidence. It came from a young man from the small town of Nazareth. This in itself took a bit of getting used to, because nobody expected a prophet to come from Nazareth. But this man had a strange gift for interpreting the Scriptures, for explaining the Old Testament, and calling for obedience to the will of God. He traveled around the local countryside, speaking in the synagogues, along the seashore, by the roads, in the hills; always the message was the same: "The kingdom of God has come; this is the acceptable day of the Lord; the Spirit is with us again."

Since these phrases meant something special to them, the people listened with enthusiasm. The kingdom of God was the time when God would once again reign over them. The acceptable year of the Lord was the Jubilee when God would deliver them from their oppressors, return the land to them, and give them freedom. When the Spirit returned, there would be hope for the people. Once again, the people began to talk of the kingdom of God. Unfortunately, however, they were almost as bewildered as we are about the meaning of the kingdom. The kingdom they expected was not the kingdom which arrived. The kingdom they wanted was not the kingdom which Jesus proclaimed.

Thus a conflict in understandings about the kingdom was inevitable. For although the same language was used, the "pictures"—the concepts—were not the same. In Jesus' day when people talked about the kingdom, they did not always understand each other. As we examine some of their misunderstandings, perhaps some of our confusion can be partially cleared away.

Whole books have been written about the kingdom of God. Obviously we cannot exhaust the subject in this study. But perhaps we can expand and deepen our understanding so that we can better discern what God is wanting to do in our midst as we live in the kingdom of God.

1.
The Hope
of the Kingdom

"God, who gave to our forefathers many different glimpses of the truth in the words of the prophets, has now, at the end of this present age, given us the truth in his Son" (J. B. Phillips translation). In this way, the author of the book of Hebrews begins the story of God's involvement with his people. He is saying that in order to understand the Christian faith it is necessary to start somewhere other than with ourselves and our inner feelings. In fact, the story doesn't even start with Jesus. Hebrews goes back into history, long before Jesus' time, and looks at the total sweep of God's activity in salvation history. Christian faith believes that Jesus is a very special person in God's process of revelation, but the door is opened to a lot of theological trouble if Jesus is pulled out of his own religious heritage. Jesus was a person—a person unlike any other person to be sure. Yet he was a person very much like every one of us. He grew up in a home, he went to religious worship, he heard the Scriptures read and interpreted, he saw the events of life going on around him. Christians dare not separate Jesus from these elements of life or wrap him in a sterile cloak in order to protect him from human contamination.

It does not destroy the divinity of Jesus to insist that he retain his humanity. To attempt to explain Jesus outside of his own religious tradition is to misunderstand the basis for the conflict he felt with the particular way in which the Pharisees interpreted that tradition.

The Old Testament people of God based their hopes for the future upon a long list of events which began with Abraham. While they began their religious history with Abraham, we should note other references to God's activity even before that time.

Genesis 1—11 is special material and needs to be read with a basic understanding of its purpose. It tells of God's creation of humanity and of a basic desire for a relationship with these people who had been created.

Few persons have captured the longing of God for fellowship as well as James Weldon Johnson in his poem "The Creation" (*God's Trombones,* James Weldon Johnson, New York: The Viking Press, 1953, pp. 19, 20). Johnson describes the loneliness of God, even after making the sun, moon, stars, earth, and all living things. He writes:

> . . . Then God walked around,
> and God looked around
> on all that he had made.
> He looked at his sun,
> And he looked at his moon,
> And he looked at his little stars;
> He looked on his world
> With all its living things,
> And God said: I'm lonely still.
>
> Then God sat down—
> On the side of a hill where he could think;
> By a deep, wide river He sat down;
> With his head in his hands,
> God thought and thought,
> Till he thought: I'll make me a man!
> Up from the bed of the river
> God scooped the clay;
> And by the bank of the river
> He kneeled him down;
> And there the great God Almighty
> Who lit the sun and fixed it in the sky,
> Who flung the stars to the most far corner
>   of the night,

> Who rounded the earth in the middle of
>   his hand;
> This Great God,
> Like a mammy bending over her baby,
> Kneeled down in the dust
> Toiling over a lump of clay
> Till he shaped it in his own image;
>
> Then into it he blew the breath of life,
> And man became a living soul.
> Amen. Amen.

It is not appropriate to even try to build a scientific model from Johnson's poem; it was not intended to be either scientific or theological. But great numbers of people have been inspired by Johnson's ability to capture the compassion of God in his longing for companionship.

The Call for a People of God

Genesis tells of the ways in which these people whom God created responded to and rebelled against God, how they were punished, and how God kept coming back to reach out to them in love. After the flood, God tried again to establish a people who would live in community with God; once again the people wandered away. Finally, in Genesis 12 the story is picked up again with the call of Abraham.

This call is the new beginning of an older belief that God wants to have a people, a nation, who will live here on this earth in obedience to what God had revealed to them. This call is also an expression of mission, expressing that God wants to gather a people who will live in such open commitment to him that other people will see and understand what God is like. When other people experience this kind of love and community, they will be challenged to respond to God's love by joining God's people, living with them in love, and experiencing salvation in its fullest sense.

God called Abraham and his descendants to a life of obedience in order to communicate with the other peoples of the earth. Through this communication salvation would be brought to everyone. This concept of God's calling of a people for mission, through whom others would experience salvation, is important in our own understanding of the kingdom. If we believe that God is a consistent God, then his purposes today will be an extension of that same desire. God is still calling people to live together in such a vivid expression of his love that they experience the wholeness, peace, and love which is his will for all people.

The Call Confirmed

Many years later another event occurred which confirmed for Israel their belief that they held a special place in God's kingdom. Through a family feud growing out of jealousy between brothers, Joseph had been sold as a slave into Egypt. Hard times at home had increased Israel's dependence upon Egypt; eventually, they found themselves in bondage in a foreign land. After years of hard labor, God intervened on their behalf. Under the leadership of Moses, God liberated them and led them to the land of Canaan which they believed God had promised to them.

At this point in Israel's history, a very important thing happened. Once again, God tried to teach a new way for the people. As they stood ready to enter the promised land, Moses called the people together and told them: "God has been good to us. We have been led out of Egypt, we have been protected from our enemies, we have been fed in the wilderness, and now we are ready to claim this land. Because God has done all these things for us, here is what he wants us to do in response." Then Moses outlined the pattern for their new life together with God. The instructions gave guidelines for the use of the land, their primary economic resource. It was to be farmed carefully to avoid burning it out; it was to be shared in an organized manner, not hoarded by just a few. There were guidelines for economic practices within the community. People were responsible for their debts. If such debts could not be repaid within six years, they were to be canceled rather than continuing for years on end. There were instructions for labor relations. Slaves were to be treated like hired hands, in a way which maintained their human dignity. After serving for a specified number of years, slaves were to be released. This helped to keep alive the element of hope in the future. (These regulations are found in Leviticus 25 and

Deuteronomy 15 as part of the Jubilee Year observance.)

These guidelines were given so that God's people could witness to the basic nature of God by the way in which they ordered their life together. This calling of others to salvation through the witness of the corporate body of believers is one of the foundational factors in the total story of God and his people. It is as central to faith as is the concept of a loving God.

Someone once said something about what happens to the best laid plans of mice and men! We have no record that Israel ever seriously obeyed these God-given guidelines for living. When they finally settled in the land, they began to act like everyone else. They fought over control of the land, they sold people into slavery when minor debts were not paid, and they farmed the land into exhaustion. It was not long until Israel, who had been called to be a witness to the nature and love of God, was just like everyone else, and sometimes even worse. They were not aware of this, however. In fact, they began to believe that they were special people because of all that God had done for them. When they gathered together for worship, they spent little time trying to discern God's will for their lives in the present time. Instead, worship became a long recital of the glorious acts of God on their behalf in the past. And soon, this people whom God had worked so hard to prepare as a witness to the other nations became so much like the other nations that there was no difference. The witness of a new way of living together as God's people was lost.

Throughout Israel's history, God had always been their leader. God had used both men and women as leaders of the people; but everyone knew that these prophets and judges were functioning as God's agents. Israel also knew that the truly first-class, respectable nations around them had kings; so they went to God pleading for a king. We may chuckle over the foolishness of wanting to trade the leadership of God for the leadership of a king, but then we also chuckle over some equally foolish things people do today.

In spite of Samuel's arguments against such action, Israel demanded that they be given a king. Their method of selection was almost predictable. They crowned the biggest man they could find in all the kingdom, a rather timid fellow named Saul! This first king was basically a disaster. Impetuous and emotionally unprepared to handle the pressures of leadership, Saul was unable to lead a nation struggling to establish its inner identity and outer borders. When Saul died in battle, there was a short period of internal skirmishing to see who would succeed him on the throne. The sons of Saul were quickly defeated by a very capable "outsider" named David. An excellent administrator and a brilliant military strategist, David provided a basic structural solidarity for the monarchy and a solid economic footing for the future.

King David was a charismatic figure, a military leader who wrote poetry and music. He soon became one of the folk heroes of the nation. In the time of Jesus (more than 1,000 years later), the people were still expecting a descendant of David to restore the kingdom that had been such a brief, yet proud experience in their history (Acts 1:6).

This expectation that God would deliver them because they were God's chosen people ran deep in Jewish thought. But Israel's rejoicing at the reign of David was of short duration. For following David's reign, Solomon became king, and he led the nation down the road to destruction through heavy taxation and pagan worship practices.

Prophets Sound the Call Once Again

But not everyone went along with the crowd. Some people understood what God was trying to do; they saw how far they actually were from what God wanted. They began to speak out loudly against practices that ran counter to the will of God. They pointed their fingers and their sharp tongues at places where Israel was not being very obedient.

Today we know these people as prophets. In their own day people had less favorable names for them. These prophets attempted to keep the vision of justice and righteousness in front of the people. People with wealth did not like the prophetic words about sharing with the poor. People in power did not like the prophetic words about serving and leading with compassion. Everyone seemed to want the word of God proclaimed, but only if it was aimed at other people. Sometimes the result was to try to kill the prophet, rather than hear what he was saying.

For example: God had originally communicated the concept that among people in God's kingdom the land should be shared equally. But soon the more enterprising Israelites began to accumulate and hoard the land (Isa. 5:8). When Isaiah criticized the practice, he lost his post as counselor to the king. Hosea spoke out of his experience with his wife, Gomer, saying that God is a forgiving God of love and pointing out the fickleness of Israel's response to that love (Hos. 4:1-3). Amos said some very critical things about the accumulated wealth, luxurious living, and oppression of the poor which he saw in the northern kingdom (Amos 5:10-12). He was thanked for his efforts by being publicly ridiculed, then told in very firm language to go back home and never set foot in Bethel again. Jeremiah tried to raise his voice against specific injustices, saying that God cares about all people; he was thrown into a sewer and almost died before friends managed to rescue him (Jer. 38). Isaiah called on the people of God to stay away from elaborate military treaties for their security, urging them to trust only in God. But his counsel was rejected and it was hinted that he might even be a traitor (Isa. 30).

Throughout the Old Testament there is this recurrent theme: God is trying to keep alive a community of people who will live together in a way that will publicly reflect their beliefs about the nature of God. Through these Old Testament prophets God was trying to communicate to the people what wholeness and community would look like in the specific events of daily living. The prophets kept speaking this word from God, calling the people to live the will of God as it had been made known to them in the law. Calling for repentance and obedience, the prophets kept holding out the promise that God's continuing concern would someday bring better times in the future.

Hosea 2:23-24 promised that God would have pity and continue to be the God of the people even though they wandered away over and over again. Isaiah 2:1-5 promised that Israel would be strong once again, so that other nations of the world would come to her to learn of God. Isaiah also said that when the people came to learn of God, they would be peacemakers, beating their swords into plowshares and their spears into pruning hooks (Isa. 2:4). One looks with dismay at the modern linking of Christian faith with strong military security and enormous defense budgets, and wonders what such behavior is saying to the non-Christian people of this world!

How Does the Kingdom Come?

The consistent theme of hope for a new day was present throughout the message of prophetic judgment. Exactly how this new day was to come was not clear. Sometimes it was expected in a gradual sort of way. The people of God would learn about God's ways and would begin to be more faithful in their response to God. Slowly but surely the kingdom of God would emerge and spread across the land. The word of God was described as a lamp which would light the way for people to walk (Psa. 119:105).

A more prominent expectation was for a dramatic apocalyptic appearance, where radical signs in the heavens and an unmistakable direct action on the part of God would bring this kingdom into existence. During the four hundred or so years between the Old and New Testaments this dramatic expectation won out. By the time of Jesus, almost all the Jewish people were looking for God to liberate them and to bring the promised kingdom to them in a dramatic way.

This shift in understanding about the kingdom of God was very gradual and actually took many generations before it was accepted. It can be seen most clearly by contrasting the Mosaic understanding with the later Jewish expectations.

The people of God had been liberated from Egypt and brought to the promised land. Because of God's grace they were to respond with certain patterns of living together: freeing slaves, canceling debts, sharing resources, and living in close harmony with the land (Lev. 25; Deut. 15). But in Psalm 102:19-20 some of the change can be seen:

>... from heaven the Lord looked at the earth,
> to hear the groans of the prisoners,
> to set free those who were doomed to die; . . .

And also in Psalm 146:7-9:

> (the Lord) executes justice for the oppressed;
> he gives food to the hungry.

The Lord sets the prisoners free;
The Lord opens the eyes of the blind,
The Lord lifts up those who are bowed down;
. . . He upholds the widow and the fatherless.

Gradually, the responsibility of doing the will of God was returned to God. It became something which God was going to do for the people, instead of the activity of God's people in response to God's generous grace which had already been given.

Another shift can be noted. The Messiah gradually assumed the responsibility of being the agent of this change. Isaiah 42:1-7 speaks of the servant of the Lord:

I have put my Spirit upon him, he will bring forth justice to the nations (v. 1).

Isaiah 61:1-2 also affirms that the servant of God will be the one doing the will of God for the people:

The Spirit of the Lord God is upon me,
because the Lord has anointed me to bring good tidings to the afflicted;
he has sent me to bind up the brokenhearted,
to proclaim liberty to the captives,
and the opening of the prison to those who are bound; to proclaim the year of the Lord's favor . . .

Jesus Picks up the Theme

This passage from Isaiah 61 is the text Jesus cited in his hometown synagogue at Nazareth when he explained his own mission (Luke 4:18-19). By this time the kingdom of God was understood as a future thing which God was going to do for the people through the promised Messiah. So when Jesus read from this text, it greatly pleased the crowd at the synagogue. They were delighted to hear that the year of the Lord had finally come. They were anticipating a few miracles of healing and blessing as proof that what Jesus had just said was actually happening.

When Jesus sensed this misunderstanding of the kingdom of God, he gave a firm "no" to it; he reinterpreted what the concept of the kingdom should really mean. To understand what Jesus was doing, it is necessary to go back to the original Mosaic institution of the Jubilee. Many years before, the children of Israel stood ready to claim their promised land. Moses told the people: "God brought us here from Egypt and gave us this land. Because of God's grace to us, here is how we are to respond." Then Moses gave instructions about how they were to live together in the new land. Now, Jesus stands in Nazareth at the threshold of another new day and tells Israel: "God has blessed us with the promise of his Spirit. God has given us the new kingdom. Because God has given us these things, here is how we are to respond to that grace." Jesus then went back to the basic instructions given by God through Moses; Jesus reestablished those instructions as God's basic will for the people.

Jesus was telling the people that their understanding of the kingdom of God was wrong. The kingdom is not something that God is going to do for us, so that all we have to do is believe and enjoy the blessings which will flow down. Living in the kingdom means that we do the will of God as best we know it, patterning our lives according to that which is shown to us in Jesus Christ. And the reason? Because God has come to us in a new way, giving us the Spirit, bringing the kingdom of God into existence. Because God is calling us to live with the people of God in salvation, expressing that salvation in a new life of hope, of joy, and of peace.

This proclamation that the kingdom of God had come was central in the preaching of Jesus. Mark 1:14-15 says that Jesus came preaching the gospel of God and saying: "The time is fulfilled, and the kingdom of God is at hand; repent, and believe in the gospel." Matthew 4:17 and Luke 4:21 also affirm this same message.

In his own lifetime, Jesus was often misunderstood when he talked about the new meaning of the kingdom of God. While he was thinking of a new way of living and giving daily expression to the presence of God among the people, the religious people of the day often thought of military and political liberation from Rome. Thus Jesus had the major problem of presenting his new peaceful understanding of the kingdom of God without triggering a popular revolt based on the old understanding. He was not always successful, as we can see in the question John the Baptist asked (Luke 7:18-23): Is Jesus really the Messiah or should the people look for somebody else? Even after the end of his ministry, the

Paul M. Schrock

disciples themselves are not completely clear on the meaning of the kingdom; they ask Jesus if now he will set up the kingdom (Acts 1:6; Luke 19:11).

Throughout the gospel of Luke, Jesus talks with his followers about how they should order their lives because of this new relationship with God. Some, like the rich ruler, heard and decided that it was not for them (Luke 18:18-30); others, like Zacchaeus, heard and said yes to the gospel; they discovered a new freedom and joy in living that they had never known before (Luke 19:1-10).

The words used in the gospels to describe this kingdom of God do allow for some confusion. At times Jesus seemed to say quite firmly that the kingdom of God is here (Luke 4:16-21; Matt. 11:2-6); yet in other places it is still coming (Luke 12:49-53; 17:22-30). The problem can be resolved, to some degree at least, by taking a both/and stance. The kingdom is here right now, for it came with Jesus. However, the kingdom is not complete or perfect; it is still developing. Only in the future will that perfection which we all hope for become a reality. What has begun with Jesus is with us now and is our hope for the future. This continuation of life with God will be further experienced in the perfection of the future life in heaven.

2.
Love and Justice

Have you noticed how much more complicated life has become recently? For many generations, people living in one part of the earth did not have much opportunity to know about what went on in another part of the earth. People did recognize how their actions affected others living around them, but this most often dealt with basic interpersonal relationships or perhaps one small group relating to another. When something went wrong, persons or groups could generally get together and work out an acceptable solution. Sometimes the solution was peaceful, sometimes it was not, but usually the involvement was limited.

In the past decades the world has become highly industrialized, interdependent, and exceedingly complex. Although the various nations work hard at being self-sufficient, not one of them ever really succeeds. They are forced to recognize their intricate interdependence. With this dependence upon each other for raw materials, energy sources, labor, and markets, the world has had to recognize new concepts of justice as well as a greatly enlarged potential for injustice.

Sometimes irritation is felt when the church keeps reexamining its position on the issues of peace, justice, and Christian love. It is easy to feel that every time the church looks at these issues, it changes its mind; the membership then feels guilty for what they are doing and are told that they have to change.

In the past Christians were taught to love, and people worked hard at that. Justice was what the law courts meted out to people who weren't willing to work together in a spirit of cooperation. Christians believed that justice was a step below the love which they were called to practice. But now the church is being told that justice needs to be introduced into the concept of love—that God's love is founded on justice. Simply working from the motive of nonresistant love may unwittingly give support to the way things are, perpetuating the injustice which minorities or third world countries experience every day. The church is being called to move beyond merely "loving" to a ministry which actively seeks justice for the oppressed. This calls for a new level of involvement with the world; this also means that some Christians are discovering (or so they are being told) that they are among the persons who are oppressing others.

Thinking about these issues will help us focus on the close relationship between love and justice. In the process we may discover that they are more closely related than we had previously imagined.

Christian Love

Love is God's active involvement with people in creating and sustaining a community where people can live together in peace. This definition of love has several facets. In traditional theological language, for example, God's love is seen in salvation and reconciliation with others; this involves both God's love for us and our love for other people. *Justice* also belongs to God's love; justice is God's activity which tries to correct the wrongs with which people have been forced to live; justice enables people to live together in peace and equality. The attributes of love also include *peace,* which is much more than simply the absence of war and hostility. Peace involves the freedom to become all that God has created persons to be, freedom to express the full range of God-given gifts which all people have, freedom to be "at home" with God, with others, with ourselves.

Unfortunately, love and justice have generally been given very short-sighted understandings. Some people have assumed that things are fine just the way they are; for them peace means a refusal to disrupt the status quo. Such a short-sighted view fails to recognize that the status quo often perpetuates injustice on many persons. "The way things are" is unjust and oppressive for many minority groups, and they cry out for justice in the form of changes. Yet other people look at the same settings and see justice for themselves as staying in power, preserving what they already have, and continuing on with their present standards of living. This creates many potentially violent situations.

In such a predicament, how does the church define love? What should be done to bring about justice for all concerned? Those who "have" are often touchy about giving up what they have; in most cases they do not see the oppressive nature of the actions which gave them what they have. They may be willing to start now in being more just, but they want to retain the head start which they enjoy in the form of education, power, and material benefits.

A race can illustrate this predicament. Two persons are competing in a one-mile race. One person wears the normal track suit and shoes while the second runner must wear heavy fishing boots and an overcoat. The race begins. The first runner quickly gains a commanding lead. Halfway through the race the first runner has a one-lap advantage, and the injustice of the situation is obvious. So the first runner stops the race in order to work out a more equitable solution. The suggestion is made that the second runner be allowed to shed his fishing boots and overcoat and wear a track suit and shoes like the first runner. But when the second runner insists that he should be allowed to take his place beside the first runner so that the earlier disadvantage is removed, the first runner is much less inclined to agree. He believes that since both are now wearing track shoes, the race is obviously fair. He is unwilling to recognize the distinct advantage which he already has. What he sees as fair is not fair at all from the second runner's point of view.

Is it being sensitive or fair when one person or group decides that today they will start being more just in their treatment of others, without recognizing their enormous advantage from yesterday or last year? What does Christian love say to such questions?

Christian Justice

We want to look more closely at the meaning of justice and try to understand how it relates to love. Frequently love and justice are separated and seen as two very different things. Justice is applied to earthly systems such as government, economics, and business, and is interpreted as giving to every person his due, without favoritism. People get what they have coming to them, or as some would put it, "you get what you deserve."

From this viewpoint, justice is the supreme concern of the state; thus anyone who appeals to the state to act out of love for the poor is confusing love and justice. God is love; nations should be just. The implication behind this viewpoint is that love is the guiding principle for persons within the kingdom of God. But when Christians move into the work of this world, they must change their love motivation into a concern for justice since that is what the state will recognize.

But should Christians work that way? In the Scriptures the people of God are called upon to practice justice because God practices justice; God's people are to pattern their behavior according to God's nature (Matt. 5:43-48). Psalm 103:6 says that God vindicates the oppressed and the weak because he is a just God. Psalm 146:7-9 repeats this theme: "God . . . who executes justice for the oppressed, who gives food to the hungry . . . ." It was widely believed that the poor should appeal to God "to do justice for the faithful and the oppressed" (Psa. 10:18; 140:12; Hosea 14:3).

This understanding of justice lies deep in the basic character of God (Psa. 99:1-4); God delivers all the oppressed of the earth (Psa. 76:9; Jer. 9:24). Throughout the Bible God is revealed as the embodiment of justice and righteousness. Justice is the essence of God's personal character; justice is the core of God's relationship with the people.

This quality of justice appears in the lives of God's people as grace. Paul, in appealing to the Corinthian Christians

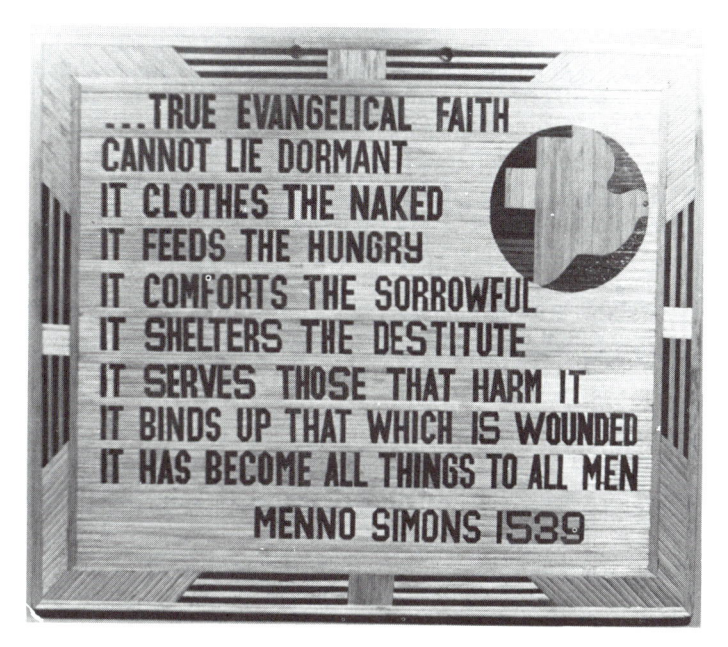

... TRUE EVANGELICAL FAITH
CANNOT LIE DORMANT
IT CLOTHES THE NAKED
IT FEEDS THE HUNGRY
IT COMFORTS THE SORROWFUL
IT SHELTERS THE DESTITUTE
IT SERVES THOSE THAT HARM IT
IT BINDS UP THAT WHICH IS WOUNDED
IT HAS BECOME ALL THINGS TO ALL MEN
MENNO SIMONS 1539

Paul M. Schrock

to share through the collection for the poor in Jerusalem, referred to this concept of justice (2 Cor. 9:8-10 is a quote from Psa. 112:9). Paul urged that the Corinthians' compassion correspond to God's compassion. They should give to the poor because God gives to the poor. Thus Paul says that the Christian should be an agent of justice in the world.

Justice is often thought of as punishment. In the Old Testament, however, that connection was not made. Justice was never used to describe God's punishment for sin. Justice was used rather in a positive sense; it referred to God's creative activity in bringing together and preserving a community of people. When this concept was picked up in the New Testament, the meaning remained the same.

Paul often used "righteousness" to explain the Old Testament word meaning justice, and he referred to the creative power of God in bringing the gift of salvation.

The justice of God is seen primarily in victory for the oppressed and the innocent. Certainly this implies judgment on the guilty and the oppressor, but such judgment is almost incidental to God's primary concern for the poor. Not that God cancels or ignores the consequences of sin. Forgiveness does not always restore health or life. When God works to bring justice in situations today, not everyone is automatically freed from the pain caused by previous actions. Persons may still have to "pay the price" for their misdeeds.

The Human Factor in Justice

We talk about wrath and vengeance as evidence of God's moral indignation. We see this vividly in war, caused by one group of people oppressing another; in pollution, caused by the oppression of nature by people who are interested in their own immediate personal comforts; we see this in starvation, caused by unjust distribution of the food supply and the resources needed to grow food.

When such situations exist among the people of the world, justice may mean that those who have gained in the past through the exploitation of others will need to do more in the future than simply stopping what they are doing. Like Zacchaeus, people may be called upon to return to the poor what has been taken from them. Zacchaeus was not forced to work at justice in this way; the confrontation he had with Jesus motivated him to do it. It was not enough to say, "From now on, I'll be good, but I refuse to discuss the implications of what I have done in the past." Zacchaeus saw the injustice of which he had been guilty and he made restitution. The response of Jesus to this activity is fascinating. Jesus declared that now Zacchaeus has experienced salvation, because he is acting like a true son of Abraham (Luke 19:9).

Such corrective justice is not punitive, not interested in "getting even." The basic concern is not punishment equal to the bad behavior of the person, but the restoration of the person to a condition of wholeness. God's justice is not intent on finding some external punishment which will correspond to the crime. At times, offenders must be restrained because their presence is a clear and present danger to the society. But even here the action should be educative and corrective, so that a person can return to society as a contributing member.

The word justice brings different ideas to people's minds, depending upon their own experience. Most Canadian and American citizens assume that the justice systems of their countries are inherently just. People who do bad things are punished; if someone is being punished, it is clear that he or she has been bad. But is this always the case? How do economic status, race, social position, and other factors affect the equal distribution of justice under the law?

A few years ago in the United States, a person of limited resources was taken to court for writing a check without sufficient funds to cover it in the bank. He explained that the overdraft resulted from a simple adding mistake in his checkbook. Since the check was for more than $50, this mistake was considered a felony; the man was sent to jail and had to pay court costs. At about the same time in another part of the country, a bank president and future United States cabinet member was regularly using overdrafts (basically the same thing as writing checks without sufficient funds to cover them) of thousands of dollars. When brought to court, he was reminded that this is not the proper way to manage finances and told that he should not do it again. With that polite reprimand, he was set free. Justice is not always as fair as many people assume it is.

Injustice inhibits and destroys authentic community. Thus the issue is not simply providing punishment equal to the crime; rather the issue becomes the correcting of injustice so that community is restored. God's initiative to correct injustice, to reconcile the parties involved, and to restore community, takes the form of grace. This restoration of community is what salvation is all about. According to the biblical record, salvation is reconciliation and restoration with God and God's people. Thus the justice which restores community is a form of salvation.

Justice in the Bible

The biblical materials become relevant as we look at justice and community. When Israel arrived in Palestine after forty years of wandering in the desert, certain guidelines for setting up their life together were given to them. The land was divided out along very specific lines, and each family had their own share (Num. 26; Josh. 18). This was understood as an expression of God's justice on their behalf. The land remained the final property of God; the people held title to it on a temporary lease type of arrangement (Lev. 25). God's concern for justice was also seen in the complicated regulations for redemption of slaves and the return of the land every forty-nine years. The community was to structure itself so that justice did not depend upon the whims of those who were in control. Justice was to be an integral part of community life.

By the time of Amos and Isaiah in the eighth century B.C., many small landowners were being taken over by more aggressive members of the community. The Jubilee year, an expression of God's creative justice which was intended to keep this kind of thing from happening, had been ignored; injustice was very common (Isa. 59:2-9; Amos 8:4-6). The period of captivity in Babylon was explained as being God's judgment on Israel for this lack of obedience to God's law (2 Chr. 36:21).

Jesus' understanding of justice will be examined in more detail later; here we will note that in his inaugural sermon at Nazareth (Luke 4:16-30), Jesus picked up this Jubilee theme with its concern for justice and said that justice is still God's will. When the people structure their lives together according to God's will, Jubilee will be their basic model. If the community of faith is to live in God's love, their corporate life will express the justice which is part of God's basic nature.

Biblical justice is thus more than the "love" which gives to less fortunate persons enough food and clothing to keep them alive, but never enough to help them resume their God-given status as contributing members of the community. Bibical justice includes both aspects: presently-needed resources and help for developing God-given potential.

One foundation for biblical justice is the activity of God. One of the more frequent phrases in the Old Testament is, "I am the Lord your God, who brought you out of the land of Egypt" (Exod. 20:2). The justice of God is always based upon the activity of God. We are not expected to do things which God has not already been doing for his people. Micah picks up this theme of justice saying that the followers of God should respond to this God of justice by doing justice in their own actions (Micah 6:8). Thus, for the Christian, justice is not based on common secular assumptions of what is right; rather it is founded on covenant justice which is based on the gracious acts of God. This is the biblical connection between God's love and justice; God's love for his people is shown in direct action which leads to justice on their behalf.

The apostle Paul echoes this same concern in a slightly different way in 2 Corinthians 5:17. He says that anyone who is in Christ is a new creation; the old has passed away and the new has come. What is the old and what is the new that has changed? Paul has been thinking about being controlled by the love of God, about not living for selfish goals; he goes on to urge the believer to be about the ministry of reconciliation. Thus Paul joins with other New Testament writers as he streses the role of each believer in helping others realize salvation.

According to Ephesians, the goal of God's plan in history is the reconciliation of all peoples and nations into one new humanity under the rule of God (Eph. 1:10; 2:11-22). This is the kingdom of God which Christ inaugurated. The church is called to bear witness to the continuing presence of the kingdom in every age. In fact, the church is the community of God's people who have pledged to live by the teachings and principles of Jesus, the acknowledged Lord of the kingdom.

Love and Justice in the Church

What does this biblical understanding of love and justice say to the church as it seeks to be faithful in its commitment to Jesus? First, the basic task of the church is to live in the power of the risen Christ, demonstrating the reality of kingdom justice in all its life. Justice is the form of love shown in that community which openly declares the Lordship of Jesus Christ. The living demonstration of authentic Christian community is the most profound witness to justice which the church can make.

This first basic task leads to the second implication. The church dare not withdraw into isolation or lose itself in cultural accommodation. It must interact with other social and political structures in order to share the reality of justice in its own life and witness. If the church loses its character as a living witness, it ceases to be truly Christian.

As the church interacts with other groups, it should give a clear witness against evil in all its forms. Nonconformity has often been thought of in negative terms as withdrawal from the world. Frequently this has meant that tacit acceptance has been given to injustice simply because the church was silent on the issue. This allowed the culture to challenge the church's claim of being a loving community of faith. Such withdrawal was seen as avoiding the issues and was detrimental to our witness and to our integrity. A vigorous witness to the gospel of Jesus Christ cannot be silent in the face of injustice.

A church which takes itself seriously as a community of God's caring people "in the world, but not of the world" will respond to the moral and legal policies of the social, political, and economic world. As much as is humanly possible, such a church will join with those who are being oppressed, becoming a living witness of love and justice, speaking a word of prophetic witness to the oppressors. Such a church will never so completely wed itself to one side of an issue that it loses its power to speak to both sides. While its actions must always be consistent with its beliefs, the church's positive witness to the gospel of love and justice may at times call for passive resistance or nonviolent disobedience to specific laws which oppress others.

As the church so acts in the Spirit of Christ, it bears witness to a hostile, fractured world that there *is* a new way —the way of peace, justice, and salvation through living under the lordship of Christ in the present realm of the kingdom of God.

3.
Signs of the Kingdom

A sign points in a direction. It is intended to help people understand something or find the way. When a sign is not read correctly, or if the sign points in a wrong direction, the result can be trouble.

Sometimes people are led astray because they are looking for the wrong signs. The biggest, flashiest sign may not mean the best family restaurant; the loudest claims may not really describe the best loaf of bread. We have been conditioned, however, to think in terms of the exceptional and the flamboyant. Signs glitter, flash on and off, rotate, change color, and do other spectacular things to get our attention.

It is understandable, therefore, that this concept of signs is sometimes transferred to the Bible. When we try to identify biblical signs, the common practice is to search for the biggest, hardest-to-explain things that we can find. We search for miracles, believing that these must be the best signs. But the Bible does not always follow that line of reasoning. The gospel of John reports a number of events which are amazing in their scope. Although they would easily fit into the common meaning of miraculous, John never uses the word "miracle" in referring to these unusual events. They are "signs" which point not to themselves but to Jesus, and they are given to help us understand who Jesus is. They are not given as firm conclusive proof but as signposts, pointing to faith.

The New Testament uses a number of different words to describe miracles. Acts 2:22 uses the three most important ones as it refers to Jesus of Nazareth, "a man attested to you by God with mighty works and wonders and signs which God did through him in your midst. . . . " The word "signs" emphasizes the purpose of the event. An event occurred to point to something else; therefore, the focus is not on the event itself, but on what it was intended to support. "Wonders" refers more to the reaction of the people to specific events; they saw these things and could not comprehend what was happening, so they wondered. "Mighty works" describes the power of God doing some particular event which could not be done easily—if at all—by natural means.

The Miracle Debate

There has always been much debate about miracles. For some persons miracle is defined as the direct intervention of God into the world, God doing things which would be impossible by any other explanation. Persons understanding miracles in this way see attempts to "explain" such events as denying the activity of God.

Tertullian, an early church leader of the fourth century, once said that a miracle "is to be believed absolutely, because it is absurd" by any other explanation, and that " . . . it is certain, because it is impossible." Although Tertullian's reasoning creates a bit of difficulty for some people today, it must be recognized that miracles do play a major role in the gospel accounts. Almost one third of the gospel of Mark, for example, is the telling of miracle stories.

Augustine, living about 1550 years ago, defined miracle as something which is not really contrary to the laws of nature, but only to our present understanding of nature. In contrast to Augustine's position, miracles have sometimes been rejected because they are contrary to the way people think life is. Such an argument assumes that nature is a rigid, completely self-contained system, in which God—an outside force—does not interfere.

In *And He Had Compassion on Them,* William Barclay

comments in support of the miracles of Jesus. First, he notes that the Jews never attempted to deny that the miracles of Jesus happened. Barclay believes that, with the hostility which the Jews felt for Jesus, they would certainly have tried to expose him as a trickster if they could have done so. But in all their attacks on Jesus, they never denied that Jesus had done some very astounding things. They did attribute to Satan what Jesus had done (Matt. 12:22-24), but they never argued that it did not happen.

Second, Barclay refers to an apology (defense) written to the Roman government by a Christian named Quadratus. Only a portion of this full document remains, but it is interesting. Quadratus writes: "The works of our Saviour were always present, . . . those who were cured were not only seen being cured . . . , but they were also always present. They remained for some considerable time, not only when the Saviour lived among us, but after he had gone from us. So much so was this the case the lives of some of them reached down to our own times."

Barclay notes that it was a serious matter to write a defense of the Christian faith to the Roman government when that same government was actively persecuting Christians. A person would hardly dare to fabricate evidence. Quadratus was in no position to make rash claims that he could not substantiate. The Roman government could easily have checked the evidence, branded him a liar, and had him punished for treachery had his claims not been true.

The Miracles of Jesus

The miracles of Jesus are generally divided into two categories. About 80 percent are healing miracles, dealing with the human body. The other 20 percent are nature-related miracles, such as stilling the storm and feeding the multitude. Many persons would say that Jesus performed these miracles to prove that he was the promised Messiah. But a close reading of the gospels indicates that Jesus did not perform miracles to please the crowd. He refused to use miracles as a way of convincing people that they should believe. Rather, miracles and signs were seen as the logical result of the dawning of the kingdom of God

(Matt. 12:28). The power of the new age was present and at work in Jesus. He performed miracles because of who he was. Miracles, therefore, are not intended to dazzle unbelievers so that they have to believe in the face of such overwhelming evidence. Miracles, rather, confirm what the believer already knows to be true: the kingdom of God is here.

Does Calling It a Miracle Make It So?

A delightful commercial used to be on television: the abbot hands a priest a stack of handwritten pages, saying that he wants one hundred copies made. The poor priest is so discouraged, thinking of the amount of handwriting this will take and the time needed to do the job. But then his eyes light up as he remembers a friend who has a Xerox copier. The friend quickly runs off the needed copies, and the priest proudly presents the finished product to the abbot, who has no idea how the work was done. He looks over the perfect copies, lifts his eyes toward heaven, and says reverently, "It's a miracle." The priest simply nods, a very mischievous grin on his face.

Was it a miracle or not? To the abbot, who had never heard of copier machines, it was; he had no other way of explaining this phenomenon except "miracle." But to the viewer who knows what copies can do and watched the priest put the pages into the machine, it was not a miracle.

We use the term "miracle" so casually in everyday talk. A baseball player makes a "miraculous" catch. Someone who is very ill recovers and we refer to the recovery as "miraculous." A student who has not been diligent in studying goes to take a test saying, "It will be a miracle if I pass."

On the other hand, we would not think of using the word "miracle" for some things that would have confounded Paul or Luke, both highly educated men in their day. If they were told of a chariot that had no horses, yet travels along the ground at 55 miles an hour, they would have called that miraculous. Yet most of us ride in a car every day and think nothing of it. And they would question our sanity if we told them about a different kind of chariot which carries hundreds of people through the air from Jerusalem to Rome in only a few hours. Yet airplanes are very common to us, not miraculous at all. Luke, the doctor, would be totally astounded to hear that it is possible to take the heart out of a person who is dead, put into another person's body, and have the second person live. But that is not called miracle today; it is simply excellent surgical technique which has been done quite a number of times.

Self-Evident Miracles?

The problem in identifying signs as they are performed is not peculiar to this age. When Jesus came announcing the presence of the kingdom of God, people were expecting one set of signs as positive proof of that claim. When Jesus did not fit those expectations, there was confusion and hostility toward him (Luke 4:28-30). This confusion over the signs of the kingdom happened at Nazareth. Jesus had quoted from Isaiah 61:1-2, which referred to the acceptable year of the Lord. He then declared that this year had arrived (v. 21).

When the local townsfolk heard this announcement, they were impressed. They began to think in the traditional ways that they had been taught. They believed that, when the acceptable year of the Lord—the year of Jubilee—came, God would perform certain deeds for the people: healing, restoring of sight, liberation. The Nazareth community was a little surprised when Jesus declared himself to be God's messenger for this acceptable year. After all, they remembered him as Joseph's son (v. 22). So they asked him for some proof to support the claims he had just made: "What we have heard you did at Capernaum, do here also in your own country" (v. 23).

Jesus, however, refused to perform miracles as a way of proving the integrity of his claim. He tried to explain to the people that their concept of the Jubilee was not totally correct. But the people would not listen to his explanations. For so many years they had been told to expect one set of signs; when Jesus came with a different approach, they could not adjust their thinking. They became angry and rejected him forcing him to leave the community.

A second example of confusion over the signs of the kingdom comes from John the Baptist in Luke 7:18-30. John

Three Lions

had been thrown into prison for speaking out against the marriage of Herod and Herodias. While in prison John reflected upon his own ministry and that of his cousin Jesus. This led him to wonder about what was happening. He sent two friends to Jesus to ask: "Are you the Messiah, or should we look for someone else?"

It seems strange that Jesus should have to answer such a question, since John had baptized Jesus less than two years before. Most likely, though, John also was expecting a Messiah who would do some of the spectacular things which Israel was expecting. When Jesus came with a soft-spoken, low profile, preaching love and forgiveness, John may have been confused.

Jesus' answer to John is interesting. He pointed to what he had been doing and gave John a report: "The blind receive their sight, the lame walk, lepers are cleansed, and the deaf hear, the dead are raised up, the poor have good news preached to them" (Luke 7:22). A comparison of this list with the earlier proclamation Jesus had made at Nazareth shows that he was doing exactly what he had claimed he would do. These specific Jubilee activities were happening to the people as promised; therefore the new age is here, and Jesus is the promised Messiah. This is the message which Jesus wanted John to get from his answer to the question.

As Jesus described what had been happening, he did not speak of what he himself was doing in a direct, personal way. The evidence for the claim that he is the expected Messiah was focused on what was happening to the people. Of course, Jesus was the one doing these things; but the best evidence he could present was to identify the themes of Jubilee which the people were experiencing.

It also becomes a challenge for us to examine the signs which are presented today as proof of the good news of the kingdom. What is the best way to communicate to others what God is doing? Is there evidence of blessing for others when someone asks for proof of the claims which are made? Or can these claims describe only internal realities of a very private nature such as forgiveness, peace, and assurance? Such personal claims are valid aspects of the gospel of the kingdom of God, for those who live in the kingdom do practice forgiveness, do live in peace, and do have the assurance of God's presence. But we need to look beyond these personal claims. When Jesus was pushed for his evidence, he turned to the people who had been healed, freed from the burden of debts, offered new life (Luke 7:22). Does the good news of the gospel primarily benefit only certain select Christian people? Or does the blessing flow through the believer to others, as Christians fulfill the gospel call to create new communities of God's people?

The Kingdom—Present and Coming

The concern over signs of the kingdom in this day sometimes takes a slightly different turn because of differing understandings of when the kingdom occurs. Not everyone agrees that the kingdom was present in Jesus. One point of view gives strong emphasis to those texts which talk of a coming kingdom,. This anticipation of a future kingdom places the primary emphasis of faith upon a future life and the present need for preparing for that future day. This viewpoint leads to a rather intense level of speculation on exactly when that day will come.

The Pharisees came to Jesus one day and asked exactly that same question: "How can we spot the presence of the kingdom?" Jesus' answer ruled out the possibility of setting up a timetable. He said that it was impossible to calculate the exact time of that day's arrival. The reason which he gave was the same as he had given in several other instances: The kingdom of God is not an external thing which will declare control of land and property and then compete with other earthly kingdoms for control. Nor is it something which God is going to do at a given point in time, so that people need to be warned to get ready. Rather, the kingdom of God is the participation of people in the ongoing will of God in the world right now—the kingdom of God is in the midst of you. The signs which the Pharisees should have been looking for were the healng of the blind and the lame, the preaching of the good news to the poor, and the message of the acceptable year of the Lord. Instead, they were enraptured with future-oriented, apocalyptic signs in the heavens.

If, as Jesus said, the kingdom is here, then the message

of the gospel is that salvation is here and now; it is not just a hope for the future. The message of the gospel is a call to join with the people of God, doing God's will as best it can be understood, and sharing in the joy of forgiveness, the blessing of a new life, and the experience of love in community with God and God's people.

Paul picks up this theme of the kingdom here and now as he declares: "Behold, now is the acceptable time; behold, now is the day of salvation" (2 Cor. 6:2). Just before these two phrases Paul referred to Isaiah 49:8, one of Isaiah's basic references to the year of Jubilee. Isaiah talks about covenant, sharing the land, setting prisoners free, feeding the hungry, and other aspects of the Jubilee message. In this Corinthian text, Paul mirrors the basic intent of Jesus that salvation has come now. At times this text has been used as a prod, urging people to "get saved while there is still time," to hurry before the door is shut in their faces. Such an interpretation severely distorts what Paul is saying. His emphasis would be just the opposite. It is not necessary to wait for some future event to experience the salvation of God, for now is the day of salvation. The blessings of salvation are available to the believer right now; come, join the people of God now. The future has been brought into this age through Jesus Christ, and all people are invited to share in that joy right now.

Paul does not teach that the salvation of God is a future reward for good behavior in this world. He was fully aware of the way in which the people of his day were looking off into the future, praying for God's day of deliverance and blessing to come to them soon. Yet, Paul taught that the day had come in Jesus the Messiah, that it was here now with all the blessings which the people were anticipating. He also acknowledged that the kingdom was not complete; there would be a final completion phase. His major thrust, however, was that in Jesus salvation has come now.

This means that the major focus of Christian living is in a faithful response in the present age, as the believer is empowered by the Spirit of God to live a holy and pure life. The Christian lives with the assurance of life after death, of some day being in the presence of almighty God; but the primary basis for faith is not the drive to do good now so that heaven is waiting after death. The biblical emphasis is upon holy living without anxiety about the future, trusting that the God who provides salvation is able to keep the promises which have been made, trusting that some day heaven will be a reality. Given this foundational trust in the promises of God, the call of faith is to live the redeeming grace of God in the present, sharing God's love with others, knowing the fullness of the joy of God's presence in the kingdom here and now.

The Signs of the Kingdom

How then are the signs of the kingdom of God to be interpreted? John asked about this, the Pharisees had questions about it, and after the resurrection the disciples still asked the wrong question about when the kingdom would come (Acts 1:6-8). Christians today look back upon the disciples and marvel at their blindness; we are convinced that if we had been there, we would have caught on very quickly to what Jesus was saying. There would have been no confusion for us.

The question which the disciples asked was a very natural one. They correctly understood the resurrection of Jesus as confirming God's decisive victory over evil. Certainly that was exactly what was to happen in the final establishment of the visible kingdom of God. On several occasions Jesus had interpreted the prophets in such a way that the disciples were led to regard the resurrection as the beginning of the final act in the drama of religious history.

The answer which Jesus gave to the disciples was a gentle correction. To their eager questions about "the end," he simply replied that they do not calculate time as God sees time; therefore they cannot understand how God is working out the final details (Luke 21). In this manner Jesus provided another caution against trying to use the Bible as a timetable for future events; Jesus indicated that people visualize time in human concepts while God sees time quite differently.

Jesus also chided the disciples' overly patriotic zeal for Israel and challenged them with a witness which would begin in Israel, but then extend over all the earth (Acts 1:8; Luke 24:47). No longer is Israel to wait for all the nations to come to her, bringing gifts to Jerusalem (Isa. 2:3; 45:14; 60:4-7); instead the witnesses of Jesus are to go out from Jerusalem to all the nations. This change in direction is crucial in understanding the biblical theme of the kingdom. Israel had expected the kingdom to be something which God was going to bring to them. But Jesus interpreted it as something his followers would take to the nations. Thus the presence of the kingdom for the church today is a serious call to mission across the face of the earth. It is never a time to relax and enjoy the manifold blessings of God which come to the church.

One of the signs of the kingdom for today would be for Christians to respond as Jesus did when asked for proof of the kingdom. Can we point to the hungry who are being fed, the naked who are being clothed, people who are finding wholeness in both body and sprit, the poor who honestly experience the good news as being pertinent to their situation? Or does the church simply reflect the common assumptions of the day and point to inner peace and tranquility, secure social standing, and material prosperity? Perhaps there has been a revival of Pharisees in the world, looking for the wrong signs and missing the real presence of the kingdom of God today.

Christ came to call people to a new way of salvation and hope. The people of God need to provide a clear call for that same salvation in their own setting.

Congregations should be communities of healing, of giving hope to the poor, of proclaiming the good news of the kingdom. They should be places where persons can be invited to experience the reality of the new kingdom in Christ. The community around the congregation should know that here is a group of persons who love and accept each other and who will give freely to others in their time of need.

What kinds of information, what attitudes, are picked up by persons who live near our congregations? Is the church fulfilling the signs of the kingdom? Or has it returned to a holding pattern of self-interest and protection from the world? The church may need to provide explanation about the signs of the kingdom so that they are properly understood. But how tragic if there are no signs to explain!

4.
Parables of the Kingdom

One day Charlie Brown, Lucy, and Linus were lying flat on their backs watching the clouds go by overhead. Lucy said, "If you use your imagination you can see lots of things in the cloud formations. What do you see, Linus?" Linus began to describe what he saw: a map of Honduras in the Caribbean; a profile of Thomas Eakin, famous painter and sculptor; the stoning of Stephen with Paul standing off to one side. Lucy was quite impressed. "That's very good, Linus. What do you see in the clouds, Charlie Brown?" Charlie, a bit overwhelmed by Linus' report, said: "Well, I was going to say that I saw a ducky and a horsie, but I changed my mind!"

There is a little bit of Charlie Brown in most people. Not everyone has the creative imagination of Linus. It is easy to see the simple and the obvious in the clouds, but it is risky to say such simple things; there is always the fear that someone else will make fun of what is said. The parables of Jesus are often approached in a similar way. Instead of seeing the horsie and the ducky that Jesus intended, people search for some profound theological detail that really is not there.

Stories—A Good Way to Teach

Wherever Jesus went in public, people gathered around

to hear what he was saying. Mark 12:37 says that the people "heard him gladly," for he told stories that were fascinating and unforgettable. Today these stories are called parables, and they indicate that Jesus was exceedingly adept at storytelling.

For centuries, Hebrew prophets and others had used storytelling to communicate moral principles in simple form. The parables of Jesus had such beauty and creativity, however, that when someone says *parable,* almost automatically attention turns to Jesus of Nazareth.

The word *parable* means "something thrown alongside of." A parable takes something which is not known and compares it with something which is widely known. Frequently a parable is introduced with a phrase like "with what shall I compare the kingdom of God" or "the kingdom of God is like . . . ." (Matt. 13:24, 31, 33, 44, 45).

The parables of Jesus were everyday stories taken from the common life of the people. Jesus was a sharp observer of human experience and many of his parables reflect this awareness of life. From these everyday observations, Jesus conveyed important lessons about what the kingdom of God is like and how people enter it. The people who heard Jesus were not always able to make the connection (Luke 8:9-10), so perhaps some degree of uncertainty is permissible in our own interpretations.

William Barclay cautions anyone who sits down to study the parables to remember that every one of Jesus' parables was produced on the spur of the moment to illustrate a point. He says that the parables are not carefully polished works of literary art. They should be seen as windows to the truth, not as solid theological dogma.

Barclay says further that parables are very effective ways of teaching. Although spoken in one time period, the story is easily adapted to all ages. Parables present the truth in pictures, and most people think in pictures, not in abstract concepts. Parables also respect the freedom of the hearer. They do not force the truth on a person; rather, they open the door for truth to be discovered. A parable says, "It is like this . . . ," or "Think of it this way . . . " and then leaves persons to draw their own conclusions. Truth which is told can quickly be forgotten; but truth which is discovered lasts a lifetime. Jesus was a master at creating situations where the hearer could discover truth.

Parables—Simple Expressions of Life and Truth

A common temptation, in approaching the parables, is to squeeze more from them than Jesus ever put there. Several observations about parables will caution against doing too much with them.

In the continued telling of parables, much of the local color describing the situation gets dropped. Only the necessary detail is given. We can be reasonably sure that the original parable form as Jesus told it included more than is recorded in the present biblical form. Having said that, however, it is important to express caution about drawing strong conclusions from what is not there.

Parable stories are generally told as one person would experience the situation. Characters come and go in the stories, but they do not take over in the story itself. Attaching great significance to secondary characters or events destroys the intent of the story. Parables are told to illustrate or stimulate thinking on one particular issue. To branch out into "other lessons which can be learned from this parable" is very dangerous.

Normally Jesus did not place value judgments on the persons in his stories. We call the Samaritan (Luke 10:30-35) "good," but that is our judgment based on how he acted. Jesus did not say whether the Samaritan was good or bad. At times, the central figures in Jesus' parables were judged as "bad" or at least as questionable. The dishonest steward (Luke 16:1-8) still baffles many people; Jesus seems to use him as an example of commendable action and does not even scold him for his original, dishonest bookkeeping.

Often parables leave the reader hanging, for frequently the stories are not finished. What finally happened to the steward? Did the Samaritan ever return to the inn? Did the sick man recover? Did the elder brother ever get over his petty anger and become reconciled to his younger brother? The stories simply do not tell us. This says that the central point of the parable is something other than the life story of these persons.

Many of the parables of Jesus describe the kingdom of God. Some of the parables which will be examined in this chapter refer to the "kingdom of heaven." Matthew uses this phrase where both Mark and Luke tend to use "kingdom of God." Basically, the two phrases are synonymous. Matthew's use of kingdom of heaven reflects the belief that the personal name "God" was too holy to be named by human beings. "Heaven" thus becomes a more general and impersonal substitute for the personal name "God."

Stories of the Kingdom
We will look briefly at some parables which open various windows to the meaning of the kingdom of God in our own time. A cluster of these kingdom parables is found in Matthew 13, with parallel accounts of some of them in Mark 4 and Luke 13.

The parable of the sower and the seed, found in Matthew 13:1-23, is explained in some detail. Comparing Luke's version with Matthew's account, we see that Jesus almost made an allegory out of it. An allegory is a story where every detail is given some symbolic meaning. Clearly, the disciples did not understand the parable and needed to ask for an explanation.

This story of the sower and the seed is built upon "end stress," or what could be called a punch line. A good bit of time is spent describing the setting, and only one sentence is given to the point of the parable. The three ways in which the seed failed to grow provide a sharp contrast for the good seed which did grow.

In good Jewish storytelling style, the three nonproductive settings are balanced by three productive harvest figures (30, 60, 100). The punch line approach puts the emphasis on the good seed and what it will do. In spite of the many reasons why some seed does not produce well, other seed does very well. This assurance that some seed will grow keeps the sower at the task.

All farmers recognize that not every grain of wheat in the field will grow. Similarly, the disciples can understand from this parable that their work will bear fruit, even though not every individual act is successful.

Since Jesus drew his illustrations from his surroundings,

most likely he did not tell this story in the city of Jerusalem. It belongs to an open, rural setting. As opposition against him began to grow, Jesus moved from the city to the countryside. The scribes were getting touchy, the Pharisees were furious (Matt. 12:9-14), and even Jesus' own family was showing concern over what he was doing (Matt. 12:46-50). Was the kingdom of God doomed to failure before it ever really had a chance? This parable spoke well to that kind of question and to that very real situation.

Jesus encouraged the disciples (and also himself?) to push on with their work, even though not everything was going well. Later, when he was alone with the disciples, Jesus gave a more detailed explanation of the story, changing the focus ever so slightly. Why don't people respond to the message? The reactions of people to the message vary because situations in life vary. The sower could not take responsibility for the fact that some of the seed did not grow. If he had stayed away from the path and the thorns to be absolutely certain that no seed would land there, he would have missed a lot of good soil next to the path. The response of others, either actual or anticipated, cannot control behavior. The work of the kingdom of God should be done in all places; disciples should not become discouraged or frustrated when some people choose not to listen or back out when things get serious. An old anonymous limerick puts it this way:

> God's Word made a perfect beginning
> Man spoiled the creation by sinning
>   We know that the story
>   Will end in God's glory
> But at present the other side's winning.

While it might be more accurate to say "it looks like the other side's winning," this limerick does describe the feelings of many people as they look at life and faith today.

The story of the sower and the seed is followed by another which uses seeds and harvest as its foundation—a story of an enemy sowing weeds among the wheat (Matt. 13:24-30). The rural folk knew exactly what Jesus was talking about, for this kind of sabotage happened. Roman law designated severe penalties for anyone convicted of sowing bad seed in someone else's land. The weed was darnel, which in its early stages looks very much like young wheat. Its root system intertwined with the wheat, making it impossible to pull out the darnel without tearing out the good wheat.

There were three ways to separate darnel from the good grain. Since darnel was not as tall as regular wheat, the persons harvesting the crop could cut off the top of the wheat, leaving the darnel standing. The field would then be burned off to kill the darnel. This made harvesting much more difficult, and some of the shorter wheat was missed in the process. A second way was for the harvesting crew to separate the darnel from the wheat and put it in separate bundles to be burned later. This was effective, but it slowed the harvesting process dramatically. If there was only a little darnel in the field, it was harvested along with the wheat and then picked out by hand before milling. Since the seed was a different color, it could easily be spotted; such sorting, however, was very monotonous work.

What does this parable mean? Remember that Jesus told the parable to illustrate an immediate issue. The immediate lesson was directed to the disciples. Jesus' disciples had a problem, even though they were not aware of it. They were worried about the kind of people whom Jesus was gathering around himself. Many people whom the world looked down upon were finding acceptance from Jesus. This was difficult for the disciples to accept, because the vision of Israel said that the Messiah would gather a new and spotless humanity. He would purge the threshing floor, gather the wheat, and throw out the chaff. The disciples must have been quite concerned over the motley multitude which thronged after Jesus. They had probably made it clear to Jesus that they expected a bit more discernment on his part about those he allowed to identify with him.

The disciples continually struggled with this question of intolerance. They saw a person casting out demons and told him to stop because he was not a member of their particular group (Luke 9:49-50). A Gentile woman came asking for help; they saw her as a pest and tried to get Jesus to send her away (Matt. 15:23). They heard the murmurings of the crowd when Jesus went to the house of Zacchaeus (Luke 19:7) and worried about the unfavorable publicity this was sure to receive.

In the face of this critical, intolerant spirit, Jesus told this story of the weeds among the wheat. He wanted to stress the difficulty in making quick human judgments about people. This parable forced the disciples to reconsider the way in which they thought about people.

People Are Still People

Before coming down too hard on the disciples, it would be good to examine some current attitudes. Could it be that persons who are part of the Jesus movement, or who are charismatic, or are too liberal, are not easily accepted because they do not fit our "standard" patterns of theology, worship, or living?

Several years ago a religious cartoon appeared in *Christianity Today;* it pictured two persons walking along a street in first-century Jerusalem. They were obviously upset about something. One said to the other, "We had such a refined group until Peter started letting in all the riff-raff!" Is that how we feel once in a while?

The church today, like Jesus' disciples, may be tempted to assume responsibility for judging people or groups who are different. In such zealous attempts to pursue a few tares, a lot of good wheat may be uprooted and condemned. Going through the kingdom of God, expelling this group because they use different phrases and words to describe their faith, expelling that group because they take a different stand on particular issues of peace and justice, expelling another group because they do something else—such action does not really aid the work of building up the body of Christ. Such action and the attitudes behind such action are destructive to all concerned. There is a lot of truth in the old rhyme:

> There is so much good in the worst of us
> and so much bad in the best of us
> that it hardly becomes any of us
> to talk about the rest of us.

This is not to deny the church's responsibility for any

discernment or discipline in Christian faith. It does provide a very clear caution to the approach which the church takes in making such judgments. Many fine Christian people may be surprised by those they find sharing heaven with them.

God Uses Small Things

Next, Matthew includes two very brief parables, telling about a mustard seed and leaven in flour (Matt. 13:31-33). These parables call us to recognize that small acts, deeds, and events can lead to something much greater.

History is supposed to be boring, or so goes the common stereotype of our day. A good history teacher, however, can turn the study of history into an exciting awareness of people and events; students begin to feel the pain, the frustration, the emotions of people who are caught up in the many small, seemingly insignificant events which eventually shape history.

When some act or event occurs, it is very difficult to comprehend what the end result is going to be. Seldom do persons know that some event will change forever the course of history. The English barons gathered at Runnymede in 1215 forced King John of England to sign the Magna Charta; few of them were thinking beyond their immediate needs of the moment. Little did they know that they were taking one of the first steps toward parliamentary democracy as we know it. When Rosa Parks decided to remain seated in a bus in Atlanta, she was simply tired. She was not intending to start a civil rights freedom movement that would change the face of America. Her one small act, however, inspired and moved others to step out for justice. Other such mustard seeds and bits of leaven continue to work in the world today.

We can look back on the events of A.D. 27-30, when Jesus was walking around as an itinerant teacher and prophet, and easily see the enormous results of God's activity in Jesus. But few people saw it that way then. What the ordinary people saw was a carpenter who had a keen insight into human nature and the Scriptures and a rare gift for storytelling. They had no idea that they were living through some of the most dramatic events in all of history.

The mustard seed and leaven parables speak pointedly to our present world where the dramatic and flamboyant seem to reign, where people are taught to "think big." Advertising constantly bombards the public with programs of anything but modest proportions. Everything is done on a huge scale. One television preacher commented that he had recently sent out a personal letter to 250,000 friends! Linking the word personal with the number 250,000 is a bit difficult to comprehend. But this approach to faith and evangelism is very persuasive; it carries a lot of weight in current religious circles. Viewers are reminded of the millions of people watching "this broadcast of the gospel," or the tens of thousands of people being reached for Jesus through this television ministry.

We should always be grateful when persons are confronted with the claims of Jesus; any criticism must be cautious and made with deep humility. Nonetheless, Christians are in danger of losing the mustard seed perspective. When persons believe that the only thing worth doing is the big thing, they can easily lose sight of the small things of the kingdom. The instinctive urge for immediate success and instant return clouds the vision and dulls our hearing of Jesus' words—words which call for the simple response of obedient faith in our own setting.

At the time he told these two parables, Jesus' ministry was not going according to the projected vision of Jewish theology. Israel's dream was of a deliverer who would liberate them from Rome in a great and glorious victory. Such deliverance would once and for all declare that they were the people of God. In contrast to this vision, the kingdom of God actually began with a prophet-like figure who walked around the countryside, teaching about God and calling for obedience to the law. The kingdom spread from a small group of twelve to an ever-expanding circle of believers. There was no great fanfare. The movement had more than its share of setbacks, but it continued to grow.

The reign of God, which began as a insignificant movement among an occupied people in a poor country, spread until it is now a worldwide communion of people. The seed has indeed grown; it has become a tree of major proportions. This figure of the tree was not new to the people of

Paul M. Schrock

55

Jesus' day. Ever since the time of Ezekiel (17:22-24; 31:3-9), the tree which shaded the wild birds of the air was symbolic of a worldwide empire which would embrace all people.

Small Beginnings Do Make a Difference

The small group which gathered that January day in Switzerland, under penalty of the state for refusing to be silent about their convictions, was primarily concerned about the question of being faithful in their present situation. While they may have hoped that a few others would follow in their footsteps, they certainly did not dream that some day people from all around the world would recognize their contribution to faith.

Alexander and Anna Margaret Mack may have hoped that others would hear their concerns and join their small community. Likely they did not dream about a group like the present-day Church of the Brethren with its far-reaching world-wide witness.

Persons who set out to organize great movements, which they expect to change the world, frequently fail. Those who attempt, instead, to be faithful to the call of God in the immediate situation often succeed far beyond their wildest dreams.

The parables which Jesus told about the kingdom call us to recognize the importance of obedience in the settings in which we find ourselves; they call us to invite others to join in that faithful and obedient walk of faith. They call for trust in almighty God and a willingness to follow God even when the way looks treacherous, believing that in Christ there is hope, security, and freedom.

5.
Lord of the Kingdom

The earliest confession of faith found in the New Testament is simply "Jesus is Lord." This does not sound very complicated. In fact, persons have often felt the need to add some detail to this confession so that everyone will know exactly what it means. The confession takes on new intensity when we recognize the critical issues raised by that simple statement.

This confession was used when the Roman government demanded a loyalty oath of "Caesar is Lord." Persons who could not make that confession were subject to instant imprisonment. In that period of history, Christians insisted that "Jesus is Lord."

The contrast between Jesus and Caesar being Lord is important for this study. Persons are not often confronted today with such a vivid choice, one which carries such obvious penalties. But in the first century, the two "lords" were seen as opposites and were placed in direct contrast with each other. Declaring "Jesus is Lord" was an affirmation of faith which rejected the ultimate lordship of Caesar and declared citizenship in a different kingdom. People made this confession of faith about Jesus in response to the political claims of Caesar over their lives.

The "Jesus is Lord" confession obviously had very intense personal meaning. But of equal importance, it was a clear statement of membership in a new kingdom. It declared that a choice had been made between the way of Caesar and the way of Jesus. To be faithful to the Scriptures, the "Jesus is Lord" confession cannot be only an inner, spiritual confession; this confession must also recognize the implications of membership in the kingdom of God.

The title "Lord" is used in some very common ways in the New Testament. Often its meaning is simply "sir." The owner of the vineyard is thus addressed (Mark 12:9), as is the person Mary supposed was the gardener (John 20:15). It was merely a polite term of address which was also used for Jesus (Mark 7:28). The disciples' use of Lord as a title for Jesus carried several levels of meaning. In Luke 9:54 it means master or leader. Both Luke and John used "Lord" in certain stories where Matthew and Mark preferred "teacher."

After the resurrection of Jesus the impact of the title changed. The term "Lord" took on dramatic new meaning, which conveyed a new depth of conviction about the person of Jesus. Since the gospels were all written after Jesus' resurrection and ascension, the writers frequently used the title "Lord" to describe events which occurred during Jesus' lifetime. So at times, the use of this term indicates that the writers saw Jesus as divine Son of God, as a special person in their midst, as God in human form. Thus, in the New Testament the title "Lord" is used in various ways and has different levels of meaning.

Human and Divine

In the gospels Jesus is presented as human, without this being a challenge to his divinity. John vehemently denounces those who do not accept the belief that Jesus was human; he claims that such people are false prophets and not of God at all. The climax to John's prologue, which begins with the assertion that God and the Word are one, ends with an equally emphatic assertion that this Word "became flesh and dwelt among us" (John 1:14). In his letters, John states Jesus' humanity even more firmly, insisting that they had seen him and even touched him with their own hands.

Why this heavy emphasis upon the humanity of Jesus? There was a widespread belief going around that Jesus was not really human after all. Persons claimed that he was really divine and only appeared to be human. This human appearance was necessary because human beings could not see Jesus unless he appeared to them as being human. The reality was, though, that Jesus was divine, because God could not be human. The early church took a firm stand against such a point of view. They insisted that Jesus was fully human just as he was fully divine; he was able to identify with the humanness of men and women, and thus demonstrate the possibility of new life for believers. While it may be easy to think about Jesus as partly human and partly divine, such a 50/50 approach will not stand the scrutiny of the Scriptures. There Jesus is 100 percent human and 100 percent divine, and no one seemed to worry about how it could be explained in detail!

The religious world today is plagued with the same kind of heresy. The divine activity of Jesus receives such a heavy emphasis that little attention is given to the reality of his humanity. The popular doctrines of salvation demand a very Godly Jesus, who is really not like us at all. The problem is complex; it is like hearing from only one child the account of a quarrel between two children. The statements sound right and make sense and seem to represent the truth. Then the other child has a chance to tell the story. It becomes obvious that "true statements" don't always tell all the truth!

While in graduate school, I taught a class in New Testament theology. One student was quite insistent that God sent Jesus to die for our sins and that whatever else Jesus might have done was relatively unimportant. She was especially upset when the class used valuable time to discuss the teachings of Jesus; she felt that they were basically unimportant for our salvation. She recognized that in order to die, Jesus first had to live, and this was the reason we have the accounts of his life. The life of Jesus, however, had no real connection with his death or with our own lives as his followers. She did not like the word followers either; in her mind Christians do not follow Jesus, they just believe in him as Lord!

This example raises important questions about the Lordship of Jesus. *How* is he Lord? What does it mean for the Christian today that Jesus is Lord? How does the cross fit into Christian beliefs about Jesus as Lord?

Why did Jesus die? Was it merely because God needed someone to be a sacrifice for sin? Was it because Jesus lived such a perfect life of loving concern for the poor and the weak that he died a martyr to the cause of peace and love and justice like many earlier prophets? Why did Jesus end up on a cross? And what does the answer to that question say about the direction for the lives of Christians today?

The Historical Context

To understand Jesus and the reason for his life and death, we will look in more detail at his life; we need to see Jesus in proper historical and religious context. Remember that the Bible teaches that Jesus was God come to earth as a human being, and human beings live at a given time and place in history.

Most Christians know little about the period of three to four hundred years between the Old and New Testaments. It is often skipped over, and we miss the impact it had upon the life of Jesus and the help it offers in understanding his ministry.

At this time, Palestine was ruled by foreigners. The Assyrians, the Egyptians, the Greeks, and the Romans all dominated the culture at one time or another during this period. Each attempted to force its own cultural and religious practices upon the Jewish people. A more blatant attempt was made in 167 B.C. when the Greeks desecrated the altar in Jerusalem by sacrificing a pig on it. They organized temple worship and tried to prohibit the study of the Torah. The Maccabee family revolted and led the nation in a holy war which succeeded in driving the Greeks out; for one hundred years there was relative peace. But in 63 B.C. Rome conquered the land with a vengeance. Large amounts of land were confiscated and Jewish owners became tenants who lived on the edge of poverty. Taxes were oppressive and religious practices were often disrupted.

In this setting, it is not surprising that the Jews looked to God for a deliverer who would drive out the hated Romans.

The Jewish Scriptures had several images for this redeemer. One image was of a deliverer, who would come from the heavens with a host of angels, destroy the enemies of Israel, and establish the eternal kingdom of God. A second theme promised the return of a warrior king like David; he would rally an army and drive out the enemy in a series of glorious victories. The third image was that of a prophet-servant who would suffer with Israel in their pain.

In our own day many people despair at the willingness of the nations of the earth to grasp at military solutions for every problem, without giving serious attention to other options. So we should not be too surprised to discover that the first century Jewish community was doing the same thing. Their Scriptures presented three options for a deliverer; they combined the messenger from God with the military general and waited for their glorious military deliverance.

The Roman government knew of these military messianic expectations. They took a very dim view of anyone who sounded even faintly like a Messiah. During Jesus' boyhood there were several armed revolts against Rome; these revolts were led by men who claimed to be the Messiah. Because of its Zealot activity, the little town of Sepphoris, just three miles from Jesus' hometown, was completely obliterated by Rome. In the attempt to maintain order, Rome crucified thousands of people.

During the lifetime of Jesus an active, underground guerrilla movement existed; its members, called Zealots, saw guerrilla activity as the way to liberate Palestine. The Sadducees and the Jewish aristocracy preferred to work out ways of accommodation with Rome. They paid huge bribes out of the temple treasury to Roman officials. The Pharisees' answer was to make faith a rigid, highly personal system of behavior in which persons could faithfully keep the law and, at the same time, avoid conflict with Rome. The Essenes decided that the entire system was so completely heathen that there was nothing left to do but leave. They withdrew to the hills of Palestine to maintain their purity and await God's divine deliverance.

A New Option

Attempts have been made to explain Jesus' relationship

to each of these movements; it seems most consistent with the gospel accounts, however, to say that Jesus came proclaiming a new option—the way of servanthood and peace in the new kingdom of God. Because this way had been so overlooked in Israel's eagerness to follow military options, it sounded like a new way. John understood this "new but not new" dilemma; he described it in one of his letters:

> My dear friends, this command I am writing to you is not new; it is the old command, the one you have had from the very beginning. The old command is the message you have already heard. However, the command I now write you is new, because its truth is seen in Christ and also in you (1 John 2:7-8).

Throughout his ministry, Jesus proclaimed a new age and a new way. Although this way had been with Israel from the beginning, from the days of Moses, it had been forgotten for so long that it sounded new.

Jesus' proclamation and way challenged the other methods which were being urged on the people. Some of these groups felt threatened by the way Jesus approached certain subjects. They joined ranks to discredit him and teamed up with Rome. Eventually Jesus was crucified on the political charge that he claimed to be king of the Jews.

Jesus Takes a Stand for the Way of Peace

Since Christians claim that Jesus is Lord, it is important to see exactly what kind of Lord he is. The decision to use peaceful methods shows through at every point in Jesus' career. The way he handled various situations instructs us in how we should respond when confronted with similar situations.

When Jesus was tempted with military and political power as the way to bring in the kingdom quickly (Luke 4:5-8), he decisively rejected the suggestion that the kingdom could be set up through military violence. This says much to our own day. Almost daily the military tells the citizens of the nation that the way to bring peace is to make war. The head of the United States army chaplaincy program at the Pentagon once told a group of Mennonite, Church of the Brethren, and Brethren in Christ ministers that every person in the United States army is a committed peacemaker and shares the same conviction for peace as Mennonites and Brethren and Quakers!

When Peter confessed that Jesus was the Messiah, Jesus immediately began to redefine what being the Messiah meant; he wanted Peter to see the new approach to the kingdom and understand his peaceful mission. When Peter began to argue with the new definitions, Jesus turned on him with a severe scolding; he even asked whether Peter might be on the wrong side (Mark 8:27-34). Clearly, Jesus believed that the way of peace as a principle for kingdom living was not up for discussion.

The night before his death, Jesus faced a final crisis. The crowd came to arrest Jesus; Peter, in his frustration and desire to defend Jesus, lashed out with a sword. Again Jesus scolded Peter, repaired the damage which had been done, and called a halt to such activity on his behalf. Later that same evening, he told Pilate that a distinctive characteristic of his followers was that they do not fight (John 18:36).

As Lord of the new kingdom, Jesus did not hesitate to challenge some of the traditional beliefs held by others. On one particular occasion he pointedly rejected a popular approach in favor of a very different solution. Matthew 5:43 gives the common understanding about the treatment of an enemy in Jesus' day: "Love your neighbor and hate your enemy." While Jesus is quoting from Leviticus 19:18 for the first part of this statement, there is no Old Testament reference which either sanctions or commands hatred of an enemy. By the time of the first century, however, most Jews had heard this interpretation so often they were convinced that somewhere it must be written! The Zealots believed it was a duty owed to God to kill the enemies of God's people. The Essenes at Qumran taught that we should love all the sons of light and hate the sons of darkness.

Jesus took a different stand. The kingdom way called for love to all people, friend and foe alike. Jesus gave a specific example to show exactly what this would mean. Roman soldiers had the legal right to demand that the citizenry carry military supplies for one mile. The way in which Jesus tells the story makes it obvious that he is referring to this kind of situation. The Zealots refused to perform this or any service for the Roman military; they looked upon anyone who did as a traitor. Jesus, however, called for the oppressed person to take command of the situation, moving outside the traditional framework of forced labor into a clear witness for the new way of the kingdom. Similarly, our lives are to be controlled, not by the demands others place upon us, but by our own inner God-inspired commitment to be loving persons.

The reason for loving the enemy is not that such love will automatically turn the enemy into a friend; indeed it might not. Christians are called to love because that is the nature of God. God loves his enemies and treats them like friends; therefore the children of God are to do the same.

Resurrection Faith

What happened after the crucifixion becomes the crucial fact for proclaiming that Jesus is Lord. The resurrection finally convinced the disciples that the claims of Jesus were true. The resurrection gave proof that the new age had literally broken in upon the old. The term "Lord" became a witness to the faith, rather than simply a title of human respect.

Paul says that the cross is the center of his faith, because the true nature of God's love for all people is seen most clearly in Jesus' death on the cross (Gal. 6:14-16). Those who walk by the rule of the cross are to be assured of receiving peace and mercy. According to Paul, all other ways of searching for truth count for nothing. It is not so much that the cross makes us different; it is rather that on the cross we experience the new way of God for his people. Both James 5:10-11 and 1 Peter 2:21 tell us that Christ left us an example and that we should become for others an example of this new way in Christ.

When we so understand the specialness of Jesus and recognize his cross as the demonstration of God's way of treating enemies, then we can understand why New Testament writers urged Christians to pattern their lives after the cross of Jesus. This is not a simple philosophic principle; it is an expression of God's giving his will for the community of

Three Lions

faith. This is highlighted in Phillippians 2 where Paul presents the cross as the proper way of church harmony. Followers of Jesus are told to have the attitude which Jesus had (v. 5); they are to understand leadership as servanthood and not as domination (Luke 22:24-27).

Jesus—Lord of Kingdom and Church
We have been saying that Jesus is Lord of the kingdom. But today people think more in terms of membership in churches. Does that mean that Jesus is Lord of the church? Does the church have any direct connection with the kingdom of God? Well, that depends. Some persons would say yes, and others would say definitely not.

65

Both the kingdom of God and the church are used to describe an aspect of the mission of Jesus. The "kingdom of God" terminology appears most frequently in the gospels and is only rarely found in the rest of the New Testament. "Church" appears only twice in the gospels (Matt. 16:18; 18:17) but is found more than one hundred times in the rest of the New Testament.

The relationship between the kingdom of God and the church has been described in various ways:

1. The kingdom of God and the church are basically the same. The kingdom which Jesus proclaimed found its fulfillment in the church. The difference in terminology is nothing more than a shift in time and is not important.

2. A second point of view sees a sharp distinction between church and kingdom. The kingdom is not the church. There is no close relationship between what Jesus proclaimed during his earthly ministry and what came to be known as the church. There is a huge gap between the proclamation of the kingdom and its actual arrival; in fact, it has not arrived yet. The church is a temporary parenthesis inserted into this gap which Jesus never intended to be. The church is seen as a form of holding action until the kingdom actually comes. While the church is important and must be taken seriously, it should not be confused with the kingdom which will come sometime in the future.

This view has serious implications for the church and how it handles Jesus' teachings about the kingdom. If the church was not in the original plans of Jesus, the things which he said about the kingdom should not be transferred to the church; they should be kept in their proper place in the future kingdom. Thus it would be in heaven—not here—where Christian believers are to love their enemies. It would be in heaven—not on earth—where the other things which Jesus taught will come to pass. This approach, called Dispensationalism, is seen in the notes which are included in the Scofield Bible.

3. The most widely accepted answer is that the church and the kingdom are not identical but are very closely connected. Jesus intended to establish a new community of God's people. He saw himself as the messenger of God, coming for this purpose. Jesus organized a group of

followers; there is some historical continuity between the disciples who walked with him on earth and the church as it is now known. The book of Acts and the epistles state clearly that the church is founded on Jesus. It is difficult to give a precise moment when the church was created; it emerged rather than being created on a given day. It can, however, be connected to the period of time around the resurrection and Pentecost.

In Acts and in the epistles, the word *church* both describes a group of believers gathered in a specific place (Corinth—1 Cor. 1:2; Judea—Gal. 1:22) and is used as a more general reference to the total church (Eph. 1:22; 5:25; Col. 1:24). In each case the meaning is the same; the church is the people of God in history.

The *kingdom of God* is the rule or sovereignty of God here on earth. It belongs to all of God's history. There was a special expression of that rule in the person of Jesus. The church as the people of God continues to witness to and embody the powers of the kingdom in our own day. Therefore the lordship of Jesus extends over the church in every age.

The confession "Jesus is Lord" was crucial for the first century believer. There were times when that confession cost persons their lives. The issue is equally important today but is more complicated, because the line between the kingdom of God and the kingdom of this world is so hazy. The kingdoms of this world try to assure Christians that by saying "yes" to national concerns they are actually saying "yes" to God. The state and unfortunately many Christians assume that saying "Caesar is Lord" is synonymous with saying "Jesus is Lord." But is it?

The confession of the Christian must always be "Jesus is Lord," recognizing that such a confession may at times be in conflict with the state. In later chapters we will examine some of the distinctions which need to be kept in mind if the believing church is to be faithful in its confession that "Jesus is Lord."

6.
In the World But Not of the World

Paul's letter to the church at Philippi begins: "To all the saints who are in Christ Jesus in Philippi . . . ." Colossians, Romans, and the Corinthian letters all have similar greetings. All Christians are "in Christ" in a given location in the world. The witness to faith is always made in the context of everyday life wherever Christians happen to be living. The tension of being in Christ and in the world at the same time is always with us. In his final prayer in Gethsemane (John 17), Jesus prayed that those who are still in the world might not be of the world.

Christians have not always agreed on how it is possible to be in the world, yet not of the world. Over the generations, this concept has been defined first in one way, then in another. As no single model has ever been satisfactory to all involved, the tension remains.

Most Christians talk about being in the world, but not of the world. Although all agree that the believer is not to be exactly like everyone else, they are not sure just how that difference should be identified. Should Christians dress differently? Some do, but most do not. Should they act differently? Again, some do, but most do not. Or should they think differently? Once again, some do, but most do not.

On what issues should Christians be different? How should they live out that differentness? Among many

Paul M. Schrock

people, there is a quick tendency to think in extremes. This makes it easy to reject certain proposed options and continue living much as before. Less is heard today about worldliness than in past years. Returning to definitions of and approaches to worldliness which were used in previous generations would not be helpful for our own day. However, we do need to recognize that as Christians we live in a dual setting; each part of our lives competes for our values, our attention, and our money. Christians find themselves caught in the middle of two systems which often contradict each other. Perhaps a bigger problem is that more and more often those contradictions are not even noticed. An even more serious problem is that when such contradictions are recognized, some Christians try to hide from them or reject them as though there were no differences. In this way, Christians may become absorbed into the world without being totally aware of what is happening.

Worldliness and God's Creation

Traditionally the word "worldliness" has been used to talk about the problem of relationships to the world. Yet with all the preaching time given to this topic, few people knew exactly what was meant. At one point the English—those persons who worshiped in English rather than in German—were referred to as worldly. At other times people who had television sets or wore certain styles of clothing were worldly. Usually such identification was negative, though it was unclear exactly why. During some periods in history, the list was narrowed down to specific things which should be avoided. In this concern to avoid the worldly, however, it was easy to become a bit overzealous. Much of what was beautiful, pleasurable, lovely, and enjoyable kept appearing on the forbidden list. Such a view of being in the world but not of the world is unfortunate, for it contradicts the purposes of God in creating the world.

Perhaps what Jesus did with the idea of worldliness will contribute to our understanding. When he warned against "this world" or "this life," Jesus was referring to a spirit or attitude which saw things only as objects to be used for personal gratification. Persons who are "of the world" think that the most important things in life are personal comfort, money, power, security, instant satisfaction of wants. The culture of this day does try to convince people that this is what life is all about, that such things will bring happiness. The Bible speaks of worldliness as "minding earthly things" (Phil. 3:19) more than heavenly things. When the human concepts of peace, love, joy, forgiveness, and sharing with others are ignored, persons lose touch with the spiritual dimension of their lives. Only when this spiritual dimension is given full expression does life come even close to the full beauty and meaning which God intended it to have. When this spiritual dimension of life is expressed, then the world takes on beauty and wholeness. C. S. Lewis expressed this idea in *God in the Dock:* "Because we love something else more than this world, we love even this world better than those who know no other."

Worldliness and an Ungodly Way of Life

In the New Testament, "the world" takes on special meaning as a basic system of ungodliness. It means adopting a way of life in which people live and work for concerns which do not reflect God's nature and righteousness. Such living is the dominant spirit of this age of which Paul speaks when he urges that we "be not conformed to this world" (Rom. 12:2).

The concept of "the world" is much more elusive than has often been thought. It has been tempting to define being "of the world" as being what other people do; such definitions could approve one's own behavior while condemning the behavior of others. When persons begin thinking in these ways, feelings of superiority are not long in coming. Since "we" don't do the bad things "they" do, we are not like them. And since we are not like those who do the bad, then we must be good. Somehow pride in one's own spirituality is nearly overlooked as these lists of sins are formed. Humility has been taught and prized as a Christian virtue; to be proud has been named "worldly." This humility, however, has somehow turned into a hybrid variety of religious pride which seems quite resistant to either treatment or cure.

In 1577, a Hutterite leader named Peter Walpot brought together a series of articles explaining the Hutterite faith.

He expressed very clearly the sixteenth century Anabaptist meaning of being in the world, but not of the world. We dare not be tempted to believe that we can simply transfer Walpot's understanding of "worldliness" to our own setting; there are many differences. What Walpot said, however, can be helpful in setting direction for tackling the dilemmas of life today.

Christians and the world are as different as heaven and earth. The world is world and remains the world and acts like the world, and all the world is one world. Christians, however, are called out of the world and are required no longer to conform to the world (John 15:19; 2 Cor. 6:11ff.; Rev. 18; Rom. 12:2), no longer to be its consort (Eph. 5:3ff.), no longer to walk in its disorderly confusion (1 Pet. 4:2ff.), no longer to pull its yoke (2 Cor. 6:11ff.).

Worldlings live according to the flesh, which rules them. They believe no one is around to observe; therefore they need the sword in their realm. Christians live according to the Spirit, which rules them. They believe the Lord observes, that he is attentive; therefore they do not need the sword among themselves . . . .

To Christians an inner joy is given; they have joy in their hearts, holding to the unity in the Spirit through the bonds of peace (Eph. 4:3). The world has no peace; by sword and coercion alone it attempts to keep outward peace.

If being a Christian could be effected with words and an empty name, if Christendom could regulate itself as it desired, if what is pleasing to it were also pleasing to Christ, and if the cross were to be born solely by means of the ugly sword, then the magistracy and its subjects, yea, most of the world would be Christian. However, since man must be born anew (John 3:7), and must die in baptism to his old life (Rom. 6:3ff.), and must rise again with Christ unto a new life and the Christian walk, that cannot be the case." (*The Golden Years of the Hutterites,* Leonard Gross, Scottdale, Herald Press, 1980, pp. 203-204).

Walpot contrasts the church and the world in sharp terms. Persons writing today would probably not use such crisp distinctions; that, in itself, might be part of our problem. How has worldliness changed over the years? Were the early Hutterites correct in their firm observations, or did they overstate the case?

The Anabaptist Difference

The early Anabaptists saw their distinctiveness being in both attitude and behavior. They chose to be different from the world in such areas as baptism, the meaning of church membership, peace, and war. When members of the early groups met at Schleitheim to discuss the nature of their common faith, these were the issues they identified as being central among themselves. In some areas, they made conscious choices on how to approach a variety of problems. The introductory letter to their statement of faith said:

> ... we who have been assembled in the Lord at Schleitheim ... make known ... that we have been united to stand fast in the Lord as obedient children of God, sons and daughters, who have been and shall be separated from the world in all that we do and leave undone, and (the praise and glory be to God alone) uncontradicted by all the brothers, completely at peace. (*The Legacy of Michael Sattler,* John H. Yoder, Scottdale, Herald Press, 1973, p. 35).

Article IV of the confession speaks directly to the "separation that shall take place from the evil and the wickedness which the devil has planted in the world, simply in this, that we have no fellowship with them. To us, then, the commandment of the Lord is obvious, whereby he orders us to be and to become separated from the evil one, and thus he will be our God and we shall be his sons and daughters" (2 Cor. 6:17; *Legacy,* p. 36).

Sometimes being separate from the world also meant being separate from other religious people, including other Christians. In 1706, the edict of the Elector Palatine took a firm stand against the way Alexander Mack and others were living their faith. The edict said, in part:

> ... it is extremely urgent that this sect—which has an outward hypocritically good appearance, and is therefore much more misleading, but is in itself exceedingly dangerous—should be smothered in its first evil brood....
>
> Those who commit this evil ... are to be arrested at once without special authorization. They are to be put in prison, and as many of them as there are must be locked to wheelbarrows and kept on public work on the fortifications and common labor.... You are to publish this present gracious decree of ours in the entire city, so that everyone can conduct himself accordingly and know how to avoid trouble (*European Origins of the Brethren,* Donald F. Durnbaugh, Elgin, The Brethren Press, 1958, p. 49).

This reference illustrates what frequently happened when people determined to live holy lives, bearing witness to their separateness from the world. Others usually acknowledged the good character of their behavior, then attacked them for it, saying that it made them all the more dangerous. When the accepted patterns of life are challenged, people often get upset and lash back at those who are doing the disrupting, even though their example may be a better way.

During the persecution which followed this edict, Alexander Mack, who had inherited substantial wealth from his father, used much of his personal resources to pay the fines of persons who were arrested for their faith. Through his caring for the families of persons who were imprisoned for their uncompromising obedience, Mack's wealth was soon depleted. Because of this constant spirit of generosity for the faithful, Mack was penniless at his death.

Many other examples could illustrate the ways in which these early Anabaptist leaders and their followers witnessed to the basic distinctiveness of their faith. Many of these persons gave a remarkable witness even to their persecutors. Sometimes, however, in the cause of zealous obedience, things got out of hand. Our own church histories reveal that our past contained not only sparkling testimonies of devout faith under persecution, but also some legalistic definitions of what separation from the world should look like. On occasion, the practice so overshadowed the underlying principle that the principle was forgotten.

Years later, another step occurred. People began to reject the practice as old and outdated, with no present meaning. In this process of rejecting the practice, they also lost the original principle. When this happened, nothing was left to give expression to the separateness which had once been there. In fact, the situation was often even worse. People reacted so strongly to the now meaningless practices that they tried to separate themselves from those who still sought to express their separateness from the world. An example of such overreaction can be seen in Holland, where the Dutch ultimately reacted quite strongly to the rigid doctrines of Menno Simons' separation from the world; they plunged into a full and almost uncritical involvement in society and were soon swallowed up by the society.

The present danger is that in attempting to recover a lost ideal, the external practice may be restored without experiencing the inner reality of the principle itself. If this happens, we will be mired in a new form of legalism. As good or bad as sixteenth century models were for the sixteenth century, they are not valid for the twentieth century if they are simply borrowed without understanding their spirit and meaning for this day.

Worldliness and a Modern Separateness?

Each new age presents a new set of dilemmas for the Christian. If Christians are to be "in the world, but not of the world" right now, they need some contemporary not-of-this-world solutions. Expressions of nonconformity in the 1980s will perhaps be strikingly different from expressions used in the 1580s. In fact, 1980s expressions might be radically different from non-conformity expressions used as recently as the 1960s.

This dilemma confronts Christians in every age. How can we pattern our response to the gospel in a way that

Joyce Miller

speaks to the issues of this age? How can we avoid simply repeating the symbols of the previous age without rejecting the persons who developed those earlier symbols? How do Christians develop new symbols which will speak to the realities of this age? Since people like their present expressions of faithfulness which have given meaning to their lives, it is easier to talk about changing symbols and patterns of response than to actually change. It is always a temptation to continue a symbol after its meaning is lost. When this happens, persons wonder why the new generation does not want to accept the old symbols of separation from the world. Frequently this results in tension between the two generations about the validity of the symbols which are to be used. Such tensions are unfortunate, for the real tension ought to be between the people and the world.

It is even more disturbing when persons today are criticized for their radical expression of not-of-this-world faith. Though such expressions are similar to the radical expressions of our spiritual ancestors, persons may be criticized as though they had left the faith or gone too far out onto the fringe. That which is admired as radical faithfulness 250 years ago is not so much admired when it is practiced in our own age by our own children in our own communities.

Symbols have meaning only when they direct persons to the reality which lies behind them. Otherwise the symbols make no sense and are like signs printed in a foreign language. Unfortunately, when a group loses the reality, it often puts enormous importance upon the symbols, believing that in the symbols it has the reality as well. This may lead to a form of legalism where something is done because it is required, even though no one knows exactly why it is required. This can also lead into hypocrisy, where people believe that by keeping the symbol they are observing the reality.

In Galatians 2:20, Paul says that we are crucified with Christ, so that we no longer live only for ourselves. We live believing that Jesus loved us and gave himself for us. Anabaptist church histories demonstrate vividly this desire to live by the grace of God. The early Anabaptists saw quite clearly the evils of their own particular period, and they consciously chose to stand in opposition to these evils as they followed Christ.

Many people today are concerned to see twentieth century Anabaptists becoming more and more a part of the world economically and socially. In the process it seems they are losing the ability and will to discern what is and what is not the way of Jesus in society. When persons begin to feel at home in the world and are accepted and respected by the community, there is danger that the clarity of their vision may become clouded. These persons have a strong urge not to offend or be different from those with whom they work and live. From here it is only a small step to beginning to question whether society really is so bad. Gradually, bit by bit, the practices and values of the culture are incorporated uncritically into the Christian way of life.

In Jesus' day, the Pharisees and the Sadducees followed this approach. They recognized the conflict between the Jewish faith and the Roman government; they tried to resolve this conflict by working out a compromise. Such compromises, though, have a way of being costly in the long run. Judaism suffered badly from the Pharisee-Roman negotiations; the same thing happens today when persons and groups become overly casual in looking at the issues of life. When people try to become "of the world," they often find themselves being hemmed in by the many pressures to compromise. It is tempting to make a first small adjustment to faith in order to survive, without recognizing that the next compromise is just around the corner, and another after that. Ever so gradually the goals of society become comfortable and even seem right; finally they are accepted as being in basic harmony with the will of God.

In this way, the preservation of the way things are soon becomes a part of the Christian goal. Rather than take a biblical stance as prophetic witnesses to the state, the church backs into the position of being high priest for the state; it pronounces God's blessings on what the state does and condemns those who dare to stand in opposition to the dominant mood of the day.

The Anabaptists believed that the Scriptures taught a clear and sharp contrast between the world and the community of the redeemed. Their membership in the kingdom of God with its eternal dimensions impacted significantly their identity with any earthly kingdom. In fact, they saw the kingdom of God going in a very different direction. Their commitment was to follow the Scriptures in building this kingdom through obedience to Christ, regardless of what the nations of this earth threatened to do. Sometimes there was harmony of purpose; more frequently, however, their radical and total commitment to Jesus led them to be out of step with prevailing cultural and national values.

The challenge for the church today is not so much to repeat what our ancestors did in actual practice; our challenge is rather to rediscover the process of biblical study and to courageously apply our Spirit-led findings to our life.

Our own denominations are in danger of trying to mesh Christian faith with the pressures and values of the world; we are close to being almost completely in and of the world. Our present challenge is to learn to be "in the world" but not "of the world," so that the message of salvation and hope is not lost to those who need to hear that God is love, that there is a new way of faith in Christ.

7.
A People of Two Kingdoms

> Blessed are the peacemakers: for they shall be called the children of God.
>
> Blessed are they which are persecuted for righteousness' sake: for theirs is the kingdom of heaven.

Paul M. Schrock

When Jesus came preaching the presence of the kingdom of God and calling people to life in it by faith, a new era broke in upon the world. When the early church proclaimed Jesus as Lord, they were identifying the presence of that kingdom and urging people to live under the Lordship of Jesus Christ. With their proclamation came the formation of new communities of believers, communities which accepted the reality of the kingdom of God and were determined to make it the central focus of their lives. The proclamation of the Word and the formation of the new communities of believers went so closely together that it was impossible to separate one from the other. The resurrection of Jesus was proclaimed as proof that he was truly the Lord. The new communities living by the Holy Spirit demonstrated the Lordship of Christ visibly in history.

This proclamation of the gospel of the kingdom, both present and coming, was the missionary message of the early church. They announced that in Jesus the kingdom of God was beginning to break into history and would eventually spread over all the earth, culminating at the end of time in the eternal presence of God. The context of their announcement is important. They did not say that a new group had been formed apart from the present structure in order to be separate and protect itself against the evil influences of the day. Rather, they launched out into society, inviting others to join the new community of God's people and to make an impact upon the world for God. They did not see themselves as isolated islands of security. They were not trying to escape from the world; these first communities were open to the world; they were a living witness to what God was doing in their midst.

Salvation was understood as participation in this new community; such salvation was through faith in Jesus Christ, the Lord of the new community. People were called to leave the ways of the world and join the people of God in a new way of living. The two ways—kingdoms—were seen in sharp contrast, with one leading to death and the other leading to life. The people of the new kingdom were those who lived by the word of Jesus, believing that it was possible to do justice and live in peace with all people as a service of worship to God.

The Biblical Call to Be a People for God
Throughout history God has been calling people to repent, to leave one way of doing things and adopt a new way. Genesis 12 begins a new story of God's activity with the call of Abraham to "go forth from your country and your kindred and your father's house to the land that I will show you." Abraham set off on a new path of life in response to God's call. Similar calls came to Abraham's descendants. This basic understanding that God had called them to a new life formed one of the central pillars of Israel's faith.

The theme was renewed after God led Israel out of Egypt. God offered to Israel a covenant relationship, which called the people to a new and holy life. "If you will obey my voice and keep my covenant, you shall be my own possession among all peoples; . . . you shall be to me a kingdom of priests and a holy nation" (Exod. 19:5-6).

The purpose of the covenant was mission. By the nature of their life in response to God, Israel would be a witness to the other nations, showing God's love and mercy for all people. Israel quickly accepted the covenant, but, as is often the case today, their obedient response was sometimes missing. At times, they forgot that their covenant with God said they would be a witness to all people (Isa. 49:6; Jer. 16:19-21; Ez. 6:7, 10, 13). When they strayed thus from their mission, the prophets reminded the people of their responsibility. In fact, throughout their history, the Israelites were reminded that they were set apart as God's chosen people to be a witness to the world.

Jesus picked up this same missionary theme as he urged the Jewish people to be faithful to their calling. Jesus, however, instituted a major change in how the faithful group was to be formed. Israel had always assumed that they were forever to be the chosen people of God, regardless of what they did or did not do. Jesus redefined the chosen people of God as those who heeded God's call to live as he taught through Jesus. The task was not changed—people were still called to holy living—only the formation of the group changed.

Thus the call of the two ways is not a new theme. From the days of Abraham to the present, the gospel message has been one of repentance from the world's ways and identification with God's way; the call is to be a witness and invite others to the new way in Jesus.

But what happens to the people of the new way? Over and over again, Christians start with good intentions, determined to put into practice the noble vision of living in the kingdom of God. But as in the past, they gradually confuse the differences between God's way of peace, love, and wholeness with the world's accepted patterns of competition, greed, and destruction. The steps taken in that direction are never very big ones; usually persons are not even aware that they are moving until they arrive at some place they never intended to be.

Historical Attempts at Faithfulness

Throughout history, a steady stream of persons has taken prophetic stands in opposition to this gradual shift toward the cultural patterns of life. For the first 300 years after Jesus the whole Christian movement was subjected to periodic and severe persecution. With the emperor Constantine that all changed. Christians became the favorites and non-Christians were persecuted. The state became the protector of the church, and the church became the spiritual voice for the state. To be a Christian meant to join with the state in trying to make everything Christian. Masses of people were baptized without knowing what it really meant. Soon church and state had become so close that it was difficult to tell them apart or to know which had control over the other.

Of course, some people saw what was happening. Hermits went off into the desert to be separate and to commune with God. Monks banded together to build monasteries where they gave themselves to prayer and spiritual meditation, free from the sins and temptations of the wicked world. This separation from the world eventually led to a double standard. Instead of being a witness and calling all people to a life of holiness and prayer, the church made special saints of those who committed themselves to living the disciplined life and excused the general population from such rigorous endeavors.

Other persons put concerted effort into reviving the church. The Rule of Benedict tried to bring more integrity to monastic life in the sixth century. Gregory the Great revised worship forms in the seventh century and began a new missionary movement. In the thirteenth century Pope Innocent III called together a major council, whose purpose was to reform the church. Thomas Aquinas produced a new theological system which tried to develop a meaningful faith for the whole church. All these attempts at reform, however, were based on the assumption that the church-state union was right.

Within this false union, the sword became the missionary tool of the church, and Christians went to war against the infidel Turks in the name of God. Soon the sword was also turned upon "heretic" Christians closer home. In 1208 Innocent III declared a crusade against the Cathari Christians of France. When one naive crusader innocently asked how to tell a heretic Cathari French person from a true French believer, he was told to kill them all; the Lord would know the true believers from the heretics, and he could sort them out when they knocked on the gates of heaven!

Within this tragic approach to faith, persons continued to work for a spiritual breakthrough, laying the foundation for the Reformation which was to come. Francis of Assisi, who died in 1226, was a living reproach to the greed, wealth, and brutality of the church. Peter Waldo in the early thirteenth century felt called to study the Scriptures and apply what he read to his own life. He was joined by others who tried to share what they believed God was calling them to do. For hundreds of years these Waldensians were persecuted for their desire to be radically obedient to the Word. John Wycliff, a professor at Oxford University in England in the mid-fourteenth century, trained men in the Scriptures and sent them out to recite long passages to anyone who would listen. John Hus, a professor at Prague University, who died in 1415, was pessimistic about the possibility of reforming the state along Christian principles. He called instead for a church which was led by the Spirit, practiced discipline, witnessed, and preached the gospel. One hundred five years later, Martin Luther said that all the leaders of the Reformation were really followers of John Hus at heart.

These pre-Reformation leaders all struggled with the

issues of the kingdom of God. Most of these leaders had decided that the kingdom of God was really the state, so what they looked for was a way to improve the spiritual life of the state. The Anabaptist reformers parted company with these leaders on this issue. They believed that Christians are called to a new way in Christ, a way which often poses a sharp contrast between the state and the church. Christians who have been influenced by this tradition believe that their primary allegiance is to God; when these two systems do clash, Jesus is to be followed.

Some people believe that history repeats itself; to some extent it seems as though Christianity is experiencing a repetition of some aspects of the Reformation in Canadian and American church-state relationships. Various subgroups in Christianity are moving in the direction of legislation for religious belief and practice, which could be leading to a very subtle union of Christian faith with national goals. In the name of national interest, the church is being admonished to support such policies as heavy military spending, maintenance of middle-class values, preservation of private wealth, punishment rather than rehabilitation of offenders, and various other issues. In exchange the government protects the church from its enemies (who are assumed to be identical with the enemies of the state), grants special tax benefits to religious groups, and even punishes those whose religious convictions deviate too far from the accepted norms of the day. Though the names have changed over the centuries and the procedure is far more sophisticated today, the basic principles underlying such fusion of church and state are much the same.

Is This Where We Ought to Be?

How has it happened that Christianity has come to this position once again? What are some of the things which led to these differences among believers? Although these are not new ideas, they often sound new to each generation; it is difficult to identify the ways in which this "new" dilemma is like the ones faced by our spiritual ancestors hundreds of years ago. Therefore it is crucial that Christians study history along with the Bible so that they can understand both the principle of church-state separation and also the way in which the church has interpreted that principle.

In their understanding of faith, Mennonites and Brethren and Brethren in Christ see life being lived in the tension between two kingdoms. On the surface, many other people seem to be saying exactly the same thing. Much of what our denominations believe to be crucial for faith is exactly what others believe is crucial; thus it seems as if we are saying the same thngs. But are we?

One approach to the kingdom of God assumes that the kingdom belongs to the future. This interpretation says that the kingdom is something which will take place in eternity, in a distinct time which is separate from our present world. The purpose of the Christian church is to save souls from the destruction that is to come, so that when the end of the world comes, they will be ready to enter the kingdom of God. This is generally identified with an understanding of religious history called dispensationalism. This understanding says that there are seven basic periods—dispensations—to history, with the kingdom of God being the seventh and final dispensation. According to this system, we are presently in the sixth period, the dispensation of grace. This form of understanding history includes a strong emphasis upon the future as being quite separate from the present, and the object of faith is preparation for this future.

A second way of understanding the kingdom of God is to see the kingdom as dealing with individual spiritual experience. According to this view, Christians live on this earth where they have to deal with such practical issues as economics, human relationships, politics, sports, and family. George E. Ladd describes this viewpoint when he writes: "The kingdom of God is here, but instead of making changes in the external, political, social order of things, it is making changes in the spiritual order and in the inner lives of men and women." (*The Gospel of the Kingdom,* Grand Rapids, Eerdmans, 1971, p. 55).

In this approach to faith, what one believes, how one worships, and how one feels towards God all belong to the interests of the kingdom of God. The external day-to-day issues of war, peace, economics, racism, and poverty belong to the interests of the earthly kingdom, and the gospel does not speak in a direct way to them. As a result, decision-making in these areas is controlled more by the logical reasoning of the day than by the Spirit of God. Life is divided into sections, and the believer is able to remain loyal to both aspects of life, making decisions on the basis of two very different standards. The spiritual life is kept in close touch with God, and the physical life functions smoothly in the world. When life goes well, this is interpreted as God's material blessing; likewise, when persons do not prosper, the assumption is that they are lacking in faith.

Sitting on the Fence Is Not Allowed!

The Anabaptists rejected these various understandings of the two kingdoms as being inadequate treatments of the Scriptures. They saw too many places where Jesus spoke in the present tense about what was now happening. They also believed that Pentecost was a radically new expression of God's activity in the present age. The first followers of the risen Lord thought and spoke in terms of being part of a new movement of God that was happening at the moment. They called for people to repent, to believe, and to begin living the new life of the kingdom immediately. When Peter preached at Pentecost, naming Jesus as Lord and Messiah, he called people to leave one way of life and join in following Jesus in this new way of life (Acts 2:38-42).

The Anabaptists adopted Peter's terminology and also called people to leave the old way and follow the new way of Jesus. They believed that there were two kingdoms in the world. In the kingdom of this world, people were prepared to force their will upon others, made certain that they got what they wanted from life, held on to what they had accumulated, and protected themselves by force if necessary. These people made decisions based primarily on how everyone else was doing it or upon what would work best at the moment.

In contrast to this, the Anabaptists saw a second kingdom, of which Christ was Lord. This kingdom was almost the exact opposite of the earthly kingdom. People in this kingdom would suffer loss rather than fight, were quick to share and help others, lived simply, and expressed love at all times. Anabaptists described these two kingdoms as going through life side by side. Salvation was the decision to leave the kingdom of this world in order to live in God's kingdom. It was not possible to sit on the fence, participating in both kingdoms at the same time, because in the Anabaptists' understanding, the two kingdoms were going in opposite directions!

Is it possible to adequately describe what the new kingdom meant for these early Anabaptists so that some parallel meanings can be drawn for twentieth century believers? Such a task is difficult and always open to misinterpretation; perhaps several examples will help us understand more clearly what the kingdom meant to them.

To Follow Jesus

A first confict between the old and the new kingdoms dealt with what it meant to follow Jesus. At its heart Anabaptism was a resurfacing of the constant desire to take seriously what Jesus taught and apply it in daily living. The Anabaptists looked at the accepted popular ways of following Jesus in their day; these ways implied that the demands of Jesus were too difficult for ordinary people to follow. The Anabaptists did not agree. They believed that the earthly life of Jesus could be a guide for the life of the Christian. They saw that Jesus suffered and yet remained faithful to the will of God. Since they recognized that Jesus had promised to be with them, they were convinced that the people of the kingdom of God could also be faithful, even when they were persecuted.

How Jesus should be understood is still a problem in Christian faith. The issue is intensified by the fact that division is within the Christian faith itself; it is not just a discussion between Christians and nonbelievers. Is Jesus someone who can be followed in daily life? Can we believe that what Jesus taught is authoritative for us? Can we be confident that if we follow Jesus we are in harmony with God and will live with God in eternity? The Anabaptists gave a resounding "yes" to these questions, and their lives bore witness to the intensity of their belief in Jesus as the Son of God. In their minds, the presence of the kingdom of God challenged the believer to live in Christ now, through the power of the Holy Spirit.

Choose Ye This Day

The second conflict of the two kingdoms is the issue of personal faith. Christian faith today is often described as being highly individualistic, almost secretive—just between the individual and God. Although this is frequently called personal faith, it is more appropriately described as private faith.

Then what does personal faith mean? Throughout most of Christian history persons were not expected to make personal decisions about faith. Charlemagne drove large numbers of Gauls through a river to baptize them, an act in which they had no choice if they wanted to live. For centuries Christians have baptized babies long before they could say "yes" or "no" to the faith into which they were being baptized. The Anabaptists believed that following Jesus was a costly decision, one that had to be made by the individuals involved, not by someone else. They said that people had to be free to choose whether or not they wanted to live holy lives, whether they wanted to follow Jesus in the kingdom of God. Thus, personal faith involves personal decision, but there is nothing secretive or private about it; personal faith is open to the community of believers and is tested and nurtured by the community.

This idea is easily recognized and accepted today, for it is common in many religious traditions; however, it was quite new and dangerous in that day. Both Catholic and Protestant leaders felt that personal choice with regard to faith was a dangerous thing. They opposed such choice with vigor.

Brethren in Christ, Mennonite, and Church of the Brethren people have much in common, particularly their deep conviction about faith and their strong love of family and friends. It can be painful when someone within the immediate family decides not to say "yes" to something as important as faith. But if a commitment of "yes" to Jesus is going to have integrity, then it must be made in a context where "no" would also be possible. If people cannot say "no," then they cannot honestly say "yes" either. Thus, granting personal freedom of choice in faith issues can be dangerous; there is always the possibility of a "no" answer. Faith in Christ, however, can only be shared; it cannot be coerced. Faith in Christ must be the result of free choice. Coercion, even with the best of intentions, violates the persons who respond to faith. Persons who follow Jesus need to be aware of the tendency to pressure others to get a religious decision.

The Importance of Community

Closely connected with personal faith is the concept of community. Again the issue is present in a crucial way. From one viewpoint, faith is presented as a highly individualistic contract between a person and God. The assumption is that, once persons are saved, they will find a church where they can worship God with others who are saved. This corporate worshiping community, however, is not crucial for faith, only helpful in keeping faith strong. The Anabaptists labeled that "old kingdom" thinking and rejected it. They believed that the creation of new communities of believers was an essential element in the gospel of Jesus Christ. Persons did not stand in isolation before God; persons stood with their brothers and sisters in the faith.

Robert Friedmann has diagramed the contrast of approaches to God in his book, *The Theology of Anabaptism* (Scottdale, Herald Press, 1973, p. 81).

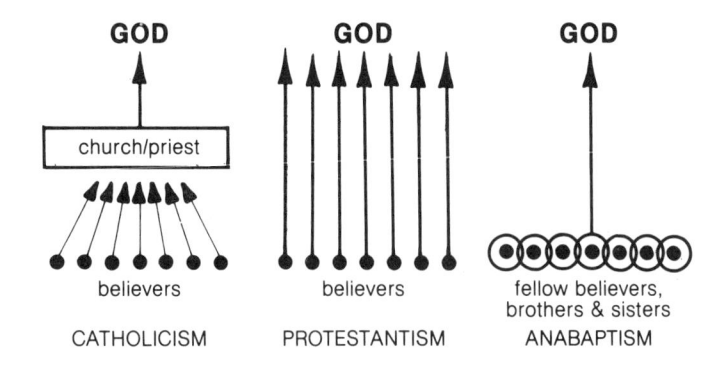

GOD	GOD	GOD
church/priest ↑ ↗↑↑↑↑↖ ● ● ● ● ● ● ● believers	↑↑↑↑↑↑↑ ● ● ● ● ● ● ● believers	↑ ◎◎◎◎◎◎◎ fellow believers, brothers & sisters
CATHOLICISM	PROTESTANTISM	ANABAPTISM

Our culture bombards us with messages saying that rugged individualism is the true expression of humanness.

Heroes are those who have made it on their own against terrible odds. In this process people are isolated into self-contained cells which promote competition rather than encourage trust and confidence. How sad that this is happening in a society where people are experiencing excessive alienation and distrust of other people and institutions—a society whose people are increasingly hostile toward each other and fearful of neighbors. Are we seeing the fruits of this earthly kingdom with its stress on competition, achievement, and individual accomplishment?

The kingdom of God invites believers to share with those who have need; it invites believers to share their own needs with others so that everyone can be helped and strengthened during difficult times. In the kingdom of God people are enhanced, encouraged, and nurtured by other persons who care about others and not just themselves. How sad that so much of what is preached as the gospel of good news serves only to promote that which is disruptive to society. People are told to go "straight to God" for their strength and support, bypassing the community of faith which God has made available as the channel of his grace and mercy.

Sharing the Good News

Jesus came preaching the presence of the kingdom of God with its new way of realizing the living reality of God in the world. He offered hope, salvation, peace, and joy in living. Society today is crying out for new visions of hope, new understandings of peace, new assurances that all has not fallen apart. Is the Christian church prepared to share the good news of the kingdom with a world that thinks it wants something else? What voices will be heard? Will we heed the cries of those who feed the fires of self-destruction, as they call for more isolation and self-protection and urge continual scrambling to find satisfaction in material things? Or are there voices in the church which will offer the freedom to trust in God, the freedom to share and love, the freedom to cooperate and give to others, and the assurance that God is with his people and watching over the future?

8. Entering the Kingdom

Bob Taylor

"What must I do to be saved?" This was the question the Philippian jailor asked (Acts 16:30). This is the question that millions of people ever since have asked. The answer to this question will be part of the discussion of this chapter. The discussion will center on several biblical situations and then note some answers given to the question in various periods of history.

Jesus came preaching the kingdom of God, calling people to live in it by faith (Mark 1:14-15). He said that salvation is found by joining the kingdom community of faith. But what instructions did he give on how persons go about entering the kingdom? What must we do to be saved?

Examples of Biblical Salvation

The words "to save" and "salvation" appear almost one hundred fifty times in the New Testament. Nearly one third of these references talk about physical illnesses and diseases, demon possession, physical death, human fears, and other physical, emotional, and spiritual problems. Being saved in the Scriptures means being made whole. Sin separates us from ourselves, from others, and from God; sin creates havoc and disharmony in every part of our lives, not just in our spiritual being. When Jesus proclaimed salvation, he was talking about the restoration of wholeness which included forgiveness of sin, restoration back into the community, and acceptance by the people of God. Membership in the kingdom of God is God's way of making this healing vivid and real in the person's life.

The account of Jesus' ministry in Mark 5 illustrates the meaning of biblical salvation. Jesus was on his way to the house of Jairus, whose daughter was sick. His journey was interrupted by a woman who had been suffering for many years. She believed that if she could reach out and touch the hem of his robe, she would be "saved." Obviously, what she had in mind was that she would be healed of a terrible twelve-year hemorrhage. She was not thinking of any profound spiritual implications for her life; she simply wanted to be made well. Although most versions of the Bible translate this phrase "I will be made well," the Greek verb is the same word which means "to be saved." When the woman reached out and touched the robe of Jesus, he turned to her and spoke: "Daughter, your faith has saved you." This is the same word the woman used earlier; once again it refers to physical healing.

As the story continues, Jesus reached the house of Jairus, where word came to them that the daughter had died. Jesus did not stop. "Do not fear; only believe and she shall be saved." Most likely, Jesus was not referring to her eternal destiny now that she was dead; rather he had something quite different in mind. He went into the house and restored the girl to her parents. Here, salvation meant restoration to life—new life—for the young girl.

What does salvation mean in these settings? For one thing, it means that our understandings need to be broadened to include more than just the salvation of our souls. To be saved includes the physical body as well as the total emotional and spiritual being. In the New Testament, to be given new life is to be saved; to be healed of a disease is to be saved.

The same word appears in another unusual setting recorded in Luke 7. Jesus was eating in the house of Simon the Pharisee. A woman came out from the crowd and poured her expensive perfume over the feet of Jesus and dried them with her hair. The Pharisee and others in the room scolded both her and Jesus for this unusual act. Jesus turned to the Pharisee and used this incident as a lesson in humility, forgiveness, and spirituality. He ended by saying to the woman: "Your faith has saved you, go in peace." Again, this is the same word as used before to mean "be well" or "be whole." What does it mean in this setting?

This usage of "saved" comes closest to what most contemporary people mean by salvation—namely, freedom from expected punishment and guilt feelings about the bad things which they have done. Thus salvation is seen as removing the consequences of past action. Because the burden of the sins of yesterday is removed, such salvation is a liberating experience. But how does this affect membership in the kingdom of God?

One common way of explaining this story is to assume that Jesus meant the woman would go to heaven when she died because Jesus had forgiven her. While that fact in itself is undoubtedly true, it is not the basic point of the story.

Jesus was confronting Simon the Pharisee with what it meant to be a kingdom member. Simon was sure that as a religious person he was in God's good graces; Jesus did not make that assumption. He told the woman she was saved because she saw the error of her ways and by actions of love and penitence indicated her desire to live a new life. Her past was no longer to be used as a control upon her in the present life. She was set free (saved) and should be treated by all as a member of God's kingdom. Jesus was not speaking about the woman's eternal destiny at death; he was describing her present condition. In so doing he contrasted her penitence with Simon's arrogance; he implied that she was a member of the people of God (and thus saved), while Simon, by his attitude and behavior indicated that he was not part of the people of God.

Another person who met Jesus and discovered new life was a tax collecter named Zacchaeus (Luke 19:1-10). Why Zacchaeus turned his back on his own people to become a tax collector we can only guess. Perhaps he saw it as the shortest route to independent personal wealth. Being a tax collector, however, had its price. Nobody liked him. Zacchaeus was an outsider in his own world. Having seen or heard of how Jesus treated people, Zacchaeus longed to meet or at least see Jesus as he was on his way through Jericho.

Jesus saw Zacchaeus perched in the tree. Much to the astonishment of the people around him, Jesus invited himself to Zacchaeus' house for a meal. We are not told much about the dinner conversation, but the results are striking. Zacchaeus did a radical about-face. Rather than continue storing up wealth for himself, he declared he would make full restitution for his past activities. His model was the Jubilee year with its restitution of property and cancellation of debts. The important thing for our study is Jesus' response to this declaration by Zacchaeus. Jesus said that Zacchaeus was in the kingdom, that salvation had come to his house because Zacchaeus was a son of Abraham.

Some people try to argue that Jesus was simply recognizing the Jewish heritage of Zacchaeus, which had been ignored by the other Jews of Jericho. This, however, would be a complete reversal of what Jesus told many other Jewish people in other settings. Jesus had been critical of those who based kingdom membership on blood ancestry (Luke 3:8). It is more accurate to believe that Zacchaeus' repentance and total change of direction with his life assured him a place in the kingdom. His behavior indicated that he was now living as a son of Abraham ought to live, doing that which God intended all good sons and daughters of Abraham to do.

Lessons From Zacchaeus

Several things about entering the kingdom can be learned from Zacchaeus. First, entering the kingdom is a conscious decision which involves repentance and a change of behavior. Entering the kingdom is an action which is taken; it is not just an attitude which only involves thinking certain thoughts about God. Christians have been deeply influenced by certain Greek philosophies which place high emphasis upon right thinking. Inappropriate actions are excused lightly by saying, "Well, it's the thought that counts." But that is not the way Jesus approached the issue. Right thoughts, or pure thoughts, are important for wholesome living; simply thinking right thoughts which are never fleshed out in specific action does not do the will of God, however. Zacchaeus did not limit himself to good thinking; he took action with his life, and Jesus commended him for it.

Second, Zacchaeus is an example of how salvation comes to a person as he responds to Jesus and his teachings. In our contemporary religious world, Zacchaeus is not often used as an example of salvation. Perhaps one of the reasons is that faith has been squeezed into a mold which tries to place every element of salvation on the cross, separating that from the teachings and ministry of Jesus. Salvation has at times been presented as acceptance of what Jesus did on the cross with little or no emphasis upon accepting what Jesus said and did before he reached the cross. In this story of Zacchaeus, however, the death of Jesus on the cross is not even mentioned. According to Jesus on this particular day in Jericho, salvation was Zacchaeus' response to the admonition to change his ways and live a new life in obedience to God. This same emphasis is also found in the Luke 18 story of the ruler who came to Jesus.

The Zacchaeus story illustrates yet a third aspect of kingdom membership. Jesus used this encounter to explain that salvation is a life-changing experience which happens now. At the beginning of his ministry (Luke 4:21) Jesus announced that the kingdom was here now. During his ministry he performed many signs which validated that claim. Here the salvation of Zacchaeus is a present reality and is based on Zacchaeus' present response to Jesus.

Salvation, Both Present and Future

This emphasis on right living is not a common understanding of salvation today. Rather, the focus is often upon accepting Jesus, which usually refers to his death on the cross. If a person so "accepts" Jesus, then he or she can be assured of a place in heaven at death. In this view, Christian faith concerns thinking about and preparation for a future home in heaven. Often this viewpoint centers on being ready to die; the religious question is, "If you were to die tonight, where would you be tomorrow?" This encourages persons to respond to Jesus out of fear of what might happen if they do not respond. Is this approach an accurate portrayal of the love of God in Jesus as it is found in the biblical story?

The biblical question of faith focuses on life, not on death. The question both Jesus and Paul ask is, "If you are alive tomorrow, whom are you going to live for?" They ask this, knowing that those who live for Jesus in this life do not need to fear the experience of death; in fact, eternal life is assured to those who walk with Jesus in this life.

Paul illustrates this understanding in 2 Corinthians 6:2. He quotes from Isaiah 49:8, a Jubilee text which talks about the radical changes of God's kingdom. Paul says, "Behold, now is the acceptable time; now is the day of salvation." Paul is not saying, "Now is your chance; get saved quickly before time runs out on you." Yet this is precisely the application made by many preachers in the public media. Quite the opposite, Paul's is a statement of joy which celebrates the fact that salvation has been brought to us here and now. The day of God's salvation, cited in Isaiah

49:8, has finally come; there is no need to wait for some future event before knowing the peace of God. The opportunity of faith has come to us in our own lifetime. Enjoy it now; live now in the peace of God's grace.

Jesus would be dismayed by an approach to salvation which tries to make deals. For example: I'll believe in you if you will get me to heaven! Reread the words of Jesus. The call of faith and salvation is constantly to "leave the way you are now going, and come follow me because by following my way, you are obeying God" (Luke 9:23; John 12:26 paraphrased).

Zacchaeus' response is all the more interesting when it is contrasted with the story of the rich ruler who asked Jesus what he needed to do to inherit eternal life (Luke 18:18-30). Jesus' answer described a way to live. When the ruler affirmed that he had honestly done all those things as best he could, Jesus did not argue with him. He simply told him: "If you want to follow me, you have to become part of the kingdom movement by doing something with your accumulated wealth. If you want to join the spiritual, new order of Jesus, you have to get rid of everything which ties you to the values and customs of the old order."

Jesus' statements to the rich ruler and to Zacchaeus must have been similar. The contrast is in their responses. Zacchaeus responded positively, took action with his wealth, and was received into the kingdom. The ruler could not quite bring himself to act. Like Zacchaeus, he had a lot of possessions. Like Zacchaeus, he wanted to do what was right. The difference between the two men is simple, yet painful. Zacchaeus responded "yes," and with a joyful and liberated spirit found new life and freedom from the old ways that controlled him. The ruler said "no" and walked away still locked into the old patterns of living.

For both Zacchaeus and the ruler the challenge was the same. In essence Jesus told both of them: "I am not playing games. What you do is your decision and you are free to choose as you wish. But if you choose to come after me, you need to know that we are in this for real. There is cost involved in being a disciple." Zacchaeus took the challenge; the rich ruler did not. As the Bible tells us, something else was more important to the ruler.

Tragically, that contrast is often no longer seen as the issue of faith. Christians are told now that they can keep their wealth and still follow Jesus. In fact, many modern religious broadcasters imply by their lifestyles and words that if one really believes, God does not ask that wealth be given away. God will continue to bless you if you only trust in him. Somewhere a great deal of what Jesus taught about salvation and entering the kingdom has been lost.

Salvation and Being Born Again

Another incident from the life of Jesus has been saved for last because it is so important. That is the story of Nicodemus in John 3. Nicodemus was a distinguished teacher who had heard some of the things Jesus was saying and was curious about them. He arranged to meet with Jesus one evening in a quiet place where they could talk. He came with a positive attitude, convinced that Jesus must be from God because of the things he had done. The problem for Nicodemus was the challenge which Jesus gave to be born again (born "from above" is the literal Greek for the phrase). Since that concept from Ezekiel 11:19 had long been neglected, Nicodemus did not recognize what Jesus was talking about. So Jesus explained. People are born into the world by natural human birth. They live in the world and they soon accept the ways of this world; soon they think and act exactly the way this world teaches them to think and act. They set their own goals, try to meet their own needs, and generally run their own lives.

Jesus said that this kind of life pattern will not allow Nicodemus to see the kingdom of God. To enter the kingdom of God, a radical new beginning is needed—a beginning as radical and complete as being born the first time. A fresh new start is necessary—a new way of thinking, indeed a new birth. Salvation in this text emphasizes the necessity of something more than just adding right religious thinking to the present approach to life. Rather than just patching up the old life, a person must enter into a new system of doing things. Jesus called for a radical new change in how persons think and act, a change in which even the basic assumptions about life must be different.

The problem today is that contemporary Christianity

has so watered down the meaning of the new birth that it has lost most of what Jesus intended it to mean. It is not that people have forgotten about the new birth as the way into the kingdom; rather, it has become a shallow and washed-out presentation that mostly refers to spiritual attitudes rather than a complete regeneration of life.

Salvation and Membership in the Kingdom

From the earliest days of Christian faith, the church has been compared to Noah's ark where all who are not inside will perish. Salvation is then seen as coming into the ark. In his sermon at Pentecost, Peter identified salvation with entrance into the new messianic community. When the people asked what they should do, Peter urged them to be baptized in the name of Jesus and join the group they had been persecuting. Paul talked about being "baptized into Christ" and being "baptized into the body of Christ" as though they were identical experiences (Rom. 6:3; 1 Cor. 12:13). In Ephesians, Paul described the salvation of the Gentiles as having citizenship with the saints and having membership in the household of God (Eph. 2:12-13).

In our day, however, salvation and being saved have been separated to some degree from membership in the kingdom of God. The focus is often on being saved from something evil, rather than a more positive salvation which focuses on relationship with God. So what exactly is the relationship between salvation and membership in the kingdom?

Salvation for the Christian begins with God reaching down to persons. Most other religions emphasize a human search for God. From the earliest days of Israel, God sought to call a people to live by his name. From the very first, salvation—the relationship of people with God—centered in a group of people, a community of faith. In the twentieth century the focus has gradually shifted away from the community of faith to the salvation of the individual soul from the consequences of sin. Private, internal religious experience is emphasized; the concept of being part of God's people, sharing together in God's grace, doing God's will here on earth, is played down and sometimes neglected altogether. As a result, many people have come to believe that the Old Testament concept of salvation involved God's calling of a people to live in relationship with him and witnessing to the nations, while in the New Testament that emphasis changed. Salvation, they believe, means being concerned about the heart and the private, inner, spiritual life of the individual. Any talk of an obedient walk with God is to be avoided, because it sounds like salvation by works. Thus the more frequently asked question is, "Are you saved?" Rather than the more biblical question, "Is Jesus Lord?"

Salvation today, however, is still identification with and membership in God's covenant community, even as it was in Old Testament and New Testament times. Any understanding of salvation which stresses only inner spiritual attitudes toward God misses much of what Jesus meant as he talked about faith as a daily living out of the message of God's love. Jesus said, "Do not think for a moment that I have come to do away with the law and the prophets. I have not come to destroy them, but to fulfill them" (Matt. 5:17 paraphrased). Or again, from the words of John in 1 John 2:7-8, "Friends, I am not giving you a new command, it is the old command you always had before you. Yet I am giving you a new commandment" (paraphrased). John is saying that this is the same story of salvation and love which God had shown from the very beginning; yet this salvation and love had been rejected for so long that when Jesus spoke of it, it sounded like something new. In actual fact, it wasn't new at all.

Entering the kingdom of God is a response to the call of faith in Jesus Christ. That action of entering the kingdom signals the intention to walk in newness of life, to turn daily life and the future over to God. The choice to enter the kingdom is the ultimate act of trust and faith in Jesus, who issues the call to follow him.

9.
Affluence and Poverty

The issue of affluence and poverty is a very sensitive one for most Christians living in the western world. They have an intellectual understanding that God is on the side of the poor, but they are not always sure exactly what that means. Although there are both poor and wealthy persons in many congregations, most of the wealthy prefer not to think of themselves in that way; they feel that they are not all that rich. In much the same way, the poor in most congregations do not recognize that even in their poverty they have much more than do the poor in most other countries. The issue is far too easily made into a polarity of "good guys vs. bad guys;" it would be more accurate to admit that almost everyone wrestles with the poverty-affluence question in ways that do not deal very responsibly with his or her own situation.

The Scriptures are clear, however, that persons who consider themselves to be members of the kingdom of God, who claim for themselves the name of Christian, must have the same concern for the poor that God has. If the church does not have an active ministry of sharing with the poor of the world, then it is challenged by the Bible in a very direct way regarding the integrity of faith. 1 John 3:17-18 says rather bluntly: "If anyone has this world's goods and sees a person in need, yet refuses to share, how can such a

Paul M. Schrock

person claim to have the love of God abiding within? My children, our love should not be just so much words and talk; it must be true love, showing itself in action" (paraphrased).

Though Christians continue to use right-sounding words and phrases, this element of concern for the poor has almost disappeared from current popular theology. This text from 1 John, however, calls for action—not simply for more committee meetings which recite pious phrases or more sermons which give "spiritual solutions."

The following incidents from Scripture will provide a basic foundation for our study of poverty and wealth and their relationship to the people of God.

The Old Testament Promise to the Poor

Christians and Jews alike look back to Abraham as a significant figure in their faith. An event from Abraham's life helps us to see how persons can overlook things they do not want to see. This incident was when Abraham tried to intercede for Sodom (Gen. 18—19). If asked why Sodom was destroyed, the great majority of Christians would say that it was because of the Sodomites' wickedness. That is correct, but what was the nature of their wickedness? Many would say that it was sexual wickedness, since sodomy is still part of our language for sexual perversion. The text, however, comments only on their great wickedness and does not identify the exact nature of their sin. The prophet Ezekiel added a later word of explanation; he wrote that God destroyed the city because the people were rich and refused to share with the poor: " . . . She and her daughters were proud because they had plenty to eat, and lived in peace and quiet, but they did not take care of the poor and underprivileged. They were proud and stubborn and did things that I hate, so I destroyed them, as you well know" (Ezek. 16:49-50 paraphrased). The text does not say that the people of Sodom overtly oppressed the poor. It says that they had lots of resources and did not help the needy, and for that, God destroyed the city.

Another Old Testament event which speaks of God's concern for the poor and the oppressed is the Exodus from Egypt. Two important things happened in the Exodus. First was the renewal of God's call of a people through whom the divine will could be made known to all people. In the Exodus event, God renewed the call that was first given to Abraham generations earlier. Second, God's action in the Exodus was designed to end the suffering and affliction of the Hebrew people. This aspect of God's activity on their behalf became a part of the confession which was repeated each year at their harvest festival: "Then we cried to the LORD the God of our fathers, and the LORD heard our voice, and saw our affliction, our toil, and our oppression; and the LORD brought us out of Egypt with a mighty hand" (Deut. 26:7-8). Israel understood the Exodus as a direct demonstration of God's opposition to the oppression which the people were enduring.

The concern for the poor, however, goes beyond redeeming people who are being oppressed. When Israel was in the process of setting a new life for herself, God gave instructions which would prevent oppression from developing among the people. The poor were to receive an opportunity to break out of their poverty. People were commanded to loan money freely to the poor (Deut. 15:7-11) and were not to charge interest for that money (Exod. 22:25). These loans were set up for six years at most with any unpaid amount to be canceled in the seventh year (Deut. 15:3). Part of the harvest was to be left in the field so that the poor could have something to eat (Lev. 19:9-10). The tithe also was an important part of the Jewish faith; one of the uses of the tithe was to provide emergency relief funds for the poor (Deut. 14:29; 16:12-13). In virtually every setting the people of God had special responsibility to care for the poor in their midst. They were given this responsibility because God had shown great compassion for them in their time of poverty and slavery in Egypt. Now they were to be God's channel of mercy to others (Deut. 24:17ff.).

This concern for the poor is very common in the prophets. During the flamboyant political and economic success of Israel in the eighth century B.C., the prophet Amos appeared; he poked beneath the shallow facade of prosperity to expose the oppression of the poor as the rich "trample the head of the poor into the dust of the earth" (Amos 2:7). He saw a court system where the rich bribed the judges, robbing the poor of any hope for fair treatment (Amos 5: 10-15). A few years later the northern kingdom fell, destroyed by God because of the mistreatment of the poor.

The southern kingdom was no better off. Isaiah declared that the rulers of Judah had acquired their wealth by cheating the poor: "The Lord enters into judgment with the elders and princes of his people: it is you who have devoured the vineyard, the spoil of the poor is in your houses. What do you mean by crushing my people, by grinding the face of the poor?" (Isa. 3:14-15). Because of such actions, Isaiah promised destruction to Judah (Isa. 3:16-26).

Jesus and the Poor

Perhaps the most important issue is how Jesus looked at poverty and wealth in his own ministry. Even before Jesus' birth, Mary sang about how God casts down the rich and exalts the poor:

My soul magnifies the Lord, . . .
he has put down the mighty from their thrones,
and exalted those of low degree;
he has filled the hungry with good things,
and the rich he has sent empty away.
>Luke 1:46-53.

When Jesus began his ministry, he emphasized God's concern for the poor and the oppressed. Jesus announced the themes for his preaching ministry by quoting from Isaiah:

The Spirit of the lord is upon me,
because he has anointed me to preach good news to
    the poor.
He has sent me to proclaim release to the captives
and recovering of sight to the blind,
to set at liberty those who are oppressed,
to proclaim the acceptable year of the Lord.
>Luke 4:18-19

Jesus then announced that the time for this activity had come. The acceptable year of the Lord was present; as God's servant, he was going to take this mission to the poor and the oppressed.

Unfortunately, most Christians today, who are neither poor nor oppressed, interpret this as referring to persons who are caught in the captivity of despair, who are poor in spiritual strength, or who are locked in by the prisons of sinful behavior and blinded by sin. This concern for the poor, as well as a concern about the rich, appears in very literal form in the basic message of Jesus too often to allow for such "spiritualizing" of the message. Matthew, admittedly, does give internal spiritual qualities to some of these concepts; this is due to the particular experience of the early church some fifty years later when Matthew was writing his gospel. Luke, however, retains the original intent and content of the message. In fact, throughout his gospel, Luke gives special emphasis to the more literal, physical realities of poverty, hunger, and oppression.

Rich Christians in a Not So Rich World

Many western Christians feel caught in a bind when they think about poverty and wealth. We know that we have more than most of the world, and therefore we are rich; we also know how much difficulty we have in paying the monthly bills for food, housing, and clothes, so that we often feel poor. When we see what some others around us have, we feel as if we are simply trying to maintain ourselves.

Perhaps this variation in wealth is the real problem. In the Old Testament, God instituted a way of organizing society which eliminated the disparity between wealth and poverty. When the time came to observe this Jubilee, however, the people who had wealth and power changed their minds; even though they knew what they were supposed to do, they decided not to share their abundance with anyone else.

There are a number of reasons why the non-poor do not want to share with the poor. The economy says that there are just a few more things we ought to have for ourselves; then we can share with the poor. Or we have this inner feeling that what we have is ours because we worked for it, fair and square, long and hard. We assume that if others would work as hard as we have worked, they would have access to the same things we have. Behind such thinking is the secret willingness to accept the culture's definition of what is needed for a "good life." This understanding of the good life urges everyone to get on the escalator which keeps wants and needs at such a high level that very few resources are left to be shared with others.

But these Christian people do care about the poor. They know the poor are there; they wish there was more to share, but it just is not there. Such Christians think about what they would do if they just had more; this successfully sidetracks them from considering carefully what is being done with the resources which are available. Christians often forget that they are not called to be faithful with what they do not have; their calling and challenge is instead to use wisely what they do have. When such wise stewardship of resources is practiced, there is the possibility of altering the approach to life so that there is more to share.

Congregational Ministries of Sharing

In our denominations, more and more people are trying to find creative ways to incorporate into their lives Jesus' teachings about wealth and poverty. They have a good heritage to draw upon. When people think about simple living or about living in community, they often turn to the Hutterites or the Amish. In their own way, these groups have maintained a long tradition of refusing to follow the prevailing patterns of society. While a study of their particular ways shows that they are not pure in their practice, it also highlights how much destructive "trinket gadgetry" the culture has forced upon the church.

Some of our congregations have set up 'agape' funds, which share congregational resources with people who have specific emergency needs. Though these funds have different names and function in different ways, the goal is the same—to assist those in need through the common sharing of the congregation. In this symbolic way, people of a congregation attempt to get around the barriers of wealth and poverty. Yet this does not actually deal with the barrier itself. In fact, many congregations do not even see such variations in wealth and poverty as a barrier to fellowship. It is simply a fact of life—and is just there. It is assumed that everyone is to be Christian, whatever the level of poverty or wealth. People take a place on one side or the other of the poverty/wealth barrier. Then they act as though the barrier is not there, or if admitting that it is present, they act as though it does not bother anyone.

Other groups within congregations have tried to raise the issue of poverty and wealth in a more open, definitive way. In small groups, they share their personal financial statements with each other; they urge that before major economic decisions are made, counsel be sought from these close and trusted friends.

Some younger members of our churches who live in towns or cities have tried to speak to the kingdom issues of wealth and poverty by consciously living in close contact with others. They share certain items in common and are available to each other as personal resources in times of stress.

Others have taken this idea one step further and joined intentional communities, such as Koinonia Farm, Reba Place, New Creation Fellowship, Fellowship of Hope, Church of the Redeemer, Jonah House, and Church of the Savior. These groups work at obedience in slightly different ways according to their own situation and vision. Their common concern is that the gospel calls Christians to share more openly and generously, both among themselves and with the poor around them.

A member of one of these communities put it rather bluntly: "If you would only take the words of Jesus about money as seriously as you take the words of Jesus about war! It is the same Jesus speaking, and he spent much more time talking about the poor and the need to love them. How dare we be selective in what words of Jesus we will obey!"

There is always the danger of making Jesus into nothing more than a prophet of economic reform. At the same time, however, if the rather blunt words of Jesus about the use of resources and the warnings about wealth are ignored, an important part of Jesus' message is not being heard.

Ideas About Wealth and Property

Ideas have a strange way of becoming part of the belief system of a people. Often these ideas begin outside of the accepted religious values; then small parts of these ideas are borrowed for daily use until gradually they become a part of the system. These concepts usually come from the culture which uses them; since Christians are part of that larger culture, they find themselves using these ideas too. As these ideas become a part of the accepted values of life, they are no longer seen as separate ideas; they are accepted as part of the religious belief system. As a final step, these ideas which originally came from a non-religious segment of society begin to dominate religious convictions and shape religious beliefs. Thus, when current economic practices are challenged, many Christians become defensive and afraid because they feel that their basic religious beliefs are being challenged.

The Bible insists that God alone has absolute ownership of property and that certain limitations are placed upon how God's people acquire and use that property. The Bible does not forbid private property. Jesus visited in Peter's house and Mary and Martha's house; there is no evidence that he scolded them for owning houses. Some of the disciples were in business for themselves or in partnership as fishermen. However, the Bible does not give owners of private property free reign to seek their own ends without considering the needs of others.

Carl F. H. Henry, a leading spokesman for conservative Evangelicalism, recently did a study in which he contrasted biblical and Roman understandings of property. He observed that Roman concepts were based on natural rights where owners had unconditional and exclusive power over property; owners could use property as they pleased irrespective of what others' needs were. In his conclusions, Henry observed that this pagan view of property "remains the silent presupposition of most of the free world's practice today." ("Christian Perspectives on Private Property," in *God and the Good,* Grand Rapids, Eerdmans, 1975, ed. C. Orbleke and L. Smedes, p. 97).

Popular Christianity is quite mistakenly proclaiming that the key to affluence is a vibrant New Testament faith. The Scriptures, however, call for the sharing of resources and teach against the accumulation of things for private security. Jesus taught a very carefree approach toward personal possessions (Luke 12:22-31). Christians are in serious danger when they assume that this permits them to be quite wealthy as long as they are not dominated by their wealth. People tend to move in a circle of friends who are similar to their own social and economic level. This makes it easy to justify a common lifestyle because it "looks average," compared to their friends. Before coming to such a conclusion, perhaps persons need to ask whether that circle of friends is large enough.

In *From the Other's Point of View,* a book filled with insight gained from cross-cultural experiences, J. Daniel Hess relates the following conversation between an American college student and her Central American host:

Enrique: You will have to pardon our humble hospitality.
Karen: Humble? I love it here. I feel quite comfortable. You are of the middle class and so am I.
Enrique: But you are rich. Your family is rich.
Karen No, not at all. We are not rich.
Enrique: What is your father's work?
Karen: My father raises pigs.
Enrique: Pigs? Oh.
Karen: I told you we weren't rich.
Enrique: But how many pigs?
Karen (stuttering): Oh, maybe two thousand, maybe three?
Enrique: Do you have a car?
Karen: Yes, an old '56 Chevy.
Enrique: Is that your only car?
Karen: Uh, we have a '73 Pontiac.
Enrique: Do you have any more cars?
Karen: My brother has one, and my dad just got a new Pontiac.
Enrique: Do you have trucks?
Karen: Yes, we have a pickup and a straight cattle truck and two semis for the farm.
Enrique: Tractors?
Karen: Yes, several.
Enrique: Well, you will have to pardon our humble hospitality.
(From the Other's Point of View, Herald Press, p. 51)

A further interesting commentary on the problems of being rich is found in Timothy:

> But those who want to get rich fall into temptation and are caught in the trap of many foolish and harmful desires which pull men down to ruin and destruction. For the love of money is the source of all kinds of evil. Some have been so eager to have it that they have wandered away from the faith and have broken their hearts with many sorrows.
>
> (1 Tim. 6:9-10 *Today's English Version*)

In this text, Paul is reflecting on a common biblical theme which began early in the Old Testament. Before the people of Israel came into the promised land, God had warned them about the dangers of wealth and what it would do to their spiritual life:

> Take heed lest you forget the LORD your God . . . when you have eaten and are full, and have built goodly houses and live in them, when your herds and flocks multiply, and your silver and gold is multiplied, and all that you have is multiplied . . . and you forget the LORD your God. . . . Beware lest you say in your heart, 'My power and the might of my hand have gotten me this wealth.' You shall remember the LORD your God, for it is he who gives you power to get wealth . . . and if you forget the LORD your God and go after other gods and serve them and worship them, I solemnly warn you this day that you shall surely perish.
>
> (Deut. 8:11-20)

Wealth usually involves things which people feel they own. Since these things belong to them, people feel a need to protect them from others who want to take them away. People even go to war to defend that which the Bible says does not really belong to them anyway!

Good Stewards of a Good Creation

Possessions can get in the way and cause trouble, but that does not have to happen. God created the world, and the Scriptures say that the creation was good (Gen. 1). The Bible does not support ascetic notions which define the virtuous as those who abstain from food or possessions. Deuteronomy 14 describes the joyous feast with which

God's people would annually celebrate the harvest. Although Jesus said a great deal about the dangers of wealth, he was certainly not an ascetic. Jesus was sufficiently fond of celebrations that some people started rumors calling him a glutton and a drunkard (Matt. 11:19). Although Christian asceticism is an ancient tradition, it did not begin with Jesus.

God's creation is good. To proclaim that principle does not go against what has already been said about the poor. Christians are called upon to live more simply, not because food, clothes, and property are evil. Rather, Christians are to live simply because other people need food to keep from starving and clothing to keep from freezing. To be poor is not a virtue; to be rich is not a sign of blessing. God would have all people enjoy the creation which he has given. It is wrong for anyone to assume that they are entitled to use however much of the creation they can corral. Prosperity without the balancing concern for biblical justice is disobedience. As God's people, we are called to be good stewards of all that God has given.

10.
Plenty and Hunger

Statistics—there are so many of them: the numbers of people who will starve this year, the numbers of people who will go to bed hungry tonight, the numbers of children who need milk. And these statistics go on and on. Perhaps that contributes to the problem. World hunger has become a set of statistics, and statistics, while impressive, are not very personal. Somehow statistics are not really people, they're just . . . statistics!

Much of our Mennonite, Brethren, and Brethren in Christ background in the western hemisphere is in agriculture. We understand the production of food and the necessity of food. We have felt a strong sense of pride about, and almost divine approval upon, our efforts to assist in feeding the world. It is more than coincidence that the origin of the Mennonite Central Committee (MCC) came into being in response to a food problem. In 1917, Mennonites received word of the tragic famine conditions in Russia. An estimated five million people died of starvation and related diseases that year, many of them our spiritual brothers and sisters. This call for help from Russia gave American Mennonites a new vision of providing food and food-growing skills for other people. It heralded the beginning of a new day in mission and world consciousness for MCC-related congregations.

It is important to recognize the two-way education that has resulted from this relief endeavor. Americans have provided some basic skills and agricultural information which improves food production. The Russians who received help provided, in turn, the challenge which led to serious re-examination of "back home" eating and living habits. They presented a new sense of reality which had to be considered. While it is not always easy to appreciate the education which other nations provide, it must be acknowledged that in this area of food and hunger, others have impacted Christian people in the western nations.

The Problem of Hungry People

Why are some people starving in the world? The quick answer might be that there is not enough food to go around. However, the Presidential Commission on World Hunger said recently that this is not the case. Malnutrition, they said, is not due primarily to the lack of food in the world. If food production were doubled, the status of the great majority of those who are hungry and malnourished would not be changed (*Washington Memo* 12:1, Jan.-Feb. 1980). People are hungry in this world because they are poor. Even when food is available, if people do not have the resources to buy it, then it is not truly available to them.

One example clarifies this problem. India frequently exports rice and wheat. When India has good harvests, there is enough food to feed their entire population. But since 30 percent of India's four hundred sixty million people are too poor to buy the food they need, they starve. Since the poor cannot buy the food, the rice and wheat is exported to wealthier countries who can pay for it. This in turn keeps the price high so that the poor in India cannot afford it. It is a strange cycle.

A Biblical Answer?

Is there a biblical perspective on the problem of hunger? Clearly, the question goes much deeper than finding a verse on this subject which can be quoted. Several texts provide examples and point to a new way of thinking about the problem of hunger in the world.

Exodus 16 provides a distinct model for food distribution.

Such a model is important because inequitable food distribution contributes significantly to world hunger. Exodus 16 describes how the children of Israel, enroute from Egypt to the promised land, encountered food problems in the desert and how God supplied their need through daily manna. Several things about this wilderness manna deserve attention.

1. The manna was a gift from heaven and not the product of any human effort.

2. Israel received the manna only in the desert where they had no resources and at a time when their faith was on the verge of giving out.

3. The bread came to them when they were seriously considering a return to Egypt with its fleshpots and abundant bread (Exod. 16:3). Therefore the manna meant more than simply food for hungry people caught in the desert. It was essential for their continued salvation.

Some observations of a different nature are also in order. Exodus 16:17-18 says: "They gathered, some more, some less. But when they measured it with an omer, he that had gathered much had nothing over, and he that had gathered little had no lack; each gathered according to what he could eat." As long as they worked on a daily basis, God provided for their needs. Those who tried to beat the system by stocking up for tomorrow lost the bread which had been collected.

This principle of provision according to need is seldom recognized today. Normally, those people with the resources also have the bread. Need has very little, if anything, to do with present distribution of food. Those who can pay get food. Those who cannot pay often go hungry.

In 1978 the east coast of Scotland was hit with a transportation workers' strike; basic food staples were coming through to the stores in limited quantities. Since no one knew just when the next truck would come through, these limited supplies were quickly bought off the shelves in large quantity by middle- and upper-income families.

In Scotland most people, especially the elderly and the poor, did their shopping every day, buying in small quantities. These people, however, could not compete with the rich; they did not have the money to buy in quantity and

Paul M. Schrock

they had no place in their tiny apartments to store large supplies of food. The empty shelves in the stores soon began to create a definite hardship for several segments of the society.

At the height of the crisis, the pastor of the St. Andrews Baptist Church preached a forceful sermon on hoarding food based on this Exodus 16 story. He outlined the problem and concluded by urging that those who had purchased extra food bring it to the church; then it could be shared with elderly members of the church and community who had serious need. He stressed that the food was to be given, not sold, to the poor. As in the Exodus story, those who had collected more than they needed should not gain any benefit from their hoarding when others were in need. I do not know exactly how much food came in; I do know that this one pastor had the insight to take the Scriptures seriously and apply them to a specific problem!

When the Israelite people were in the wilderness, only on the sixth day were they permitted to store food for tomorrow. Such preparation for the honest observation of the Sabbath was not considered hoarding. Since their food was received as a gift and there was no other food around, the Israelites took seriously these rules about food gathering and Sabbath observing. But in Israel's later history when the society moved toward success, competition, security, and force, the Sabbath observance also changed in its meaning; in fact, it almost disappeared (Amos 8:4-6). When the Sabbath was thus neglected, worship of God suffered and the symbolism behind equal food distribution was lost. Covetousness and self-preservation became dominant, first among a few individuals and then in larger groups; finally such self-preservation became a general policy of the larger society.

When Israel reached the promised land, the people began to produce their own bread. Since they were providing the food, it seemed less crucial to give thanks to God for daily bread. It also seemed appropriate to distribute the bread according to an individual's ability to pay for it rather than according to needs as had been the case in the wilderness.

Jesus Provides Bread in the Wilderness

What is the New Testament perspective on hunger? What did Jesus do with the food distribution problem? On two occasions recorded in Mark, Jesus faced a symbolic, although very real, food problem. In one account (Mark 6), Jesus fed five thousand persons; in the other (Mark 8), the number was four thousand. In each case the food was given to meet a need, with no thought of repayment. Though the disciples raised the economic question of who would pay the two hundred working days' salary needed to buy the bread, Jesus seemed unconcerned about this matter.

William Barclay suggests that the people all had a small lunch with them but, because of the size of the crowd, had decided to keep their lunches for themselves. Perhaps the problem was much like that faced today. The food is there, but if no one wants to share with the neighbor, people go hungry. When the little boy took the first step by making his lunch available, others began to share; eventually everyone had enough to eat, and there was even food left over.

How Big Should the Circle Be?

In our society persons are encouraged to look out for themselves, to meet their own needs first. They are told that the problem of food distribution is far too complex to understand. The implication is that things should continue on just as they are, that people should not trouble themselves with such matters, that those who are presently running the system should keep on running it even though it is not working very well. What goes on in the world becomes so separated from what persons do that they no longer feel any close connection or responsibility. The following progressive examples will help to clarify this situation.

John and his family are members of a local congregation. Each evening John sits down with his family to eat; he takes all the food he wants; whatever is left over, the children may have. Sometimes there is a chicken wing, sometimes a few slices of bread for the children; most often there is nothing. The children slowly lose weight and are often sick with minor ailments. At the same time John complains, in a humorous way, about having to watch the old waistline these days. Over a period of several months, two of the children are hospitalized and one dies of malnutrition. Most of us quickly see that John's actions are wrong and sinful; we would expect the church to confront him about his actions and call him to repentance and change.

Enlarge the circle just a bit. John and his family live in a community where special problems make food scarce. John is fortunate, however; he has a freezer stocked full of food and a big garden which he can afford to fertilize and water liberally. Though the neighbors are struggling to find enough to eat, John's family eats well. After dinner each evening John helps to clear off the table; he scrapes the leftover casserole, a bit of salad, and two half-eaten slices of bread into the garbage. John throws out more food than some of the neighbors had on their tables to start with.

What about such behavior? Is John still a sinner, or is he just not being sensitive to the needs of others? Should the church take their concern to John or not? Should the church even be concerned?

Enlarge the circle one more time. John and his family, with all the families in his local town, sit down at the dinner table with the whole world. John has plenty to eat, so do his neighbors . . . or do they? Who are John's neighbors? Just because people do not sit at John's dinner table or peek over his backyard fence, does that mean they are not neighbors? Is there no connection between the way John's family eats and the starvation of many people in other parts of the world?

Before you argue that the illustration is too simplistic (which indeed it is), think about the energy we use to grow, process, and store food. It is estimated that the fertilizer used in a year by western nations to keep lawns plush and golf courses green would satisfy India's fertilizer needs for one year; this would probably keep several thousand people from starving to death. If the demand for luxury fertilizer usage were lessened, more would be available for crucial food products at a lower price; this might make it possible for the poorer countries to compete. The result could be that the poverty-starvation cycle might have a few exits built into it. What is the value in human life that Americans place on a green, manicured yard or a golf course with no dry, bare spots in the fairways?

When the results of what people do are separated from the deed itself by several thousand miles, several months, or several steps in the world economic system, it is hard for persons to accept responsibility for what is done to others. That is precisely what has happened in our society. When persons do not accept responsibility for the ways in which their actions affect others, then nothing happens, nothing changes. In one place, people continue to starve; in another place, obesity and dieting are major health concerns.

Such statements are not pleasant to say or to read, and most of us certainly wish that they were not true. If we admit that they are true, then we also must realize that Satan is having more impact on the church than any of us want to admit. Does God want things to be the way they are? How that question is answered probably depends on whether the person answering it is hungry or well-fed!

A Model From Solomon's Day

As Israel began to function as a nation, some interesting things happened with regard to food distribution. Solomon built a wealthy and powerful system, based on three interdependent factors which led to its eventual collapse: affluent economics (1 Kings 4:20), oppressive labor and politics (1 Kings 5:13ff.; 9:15ff.), and religious control of God (1 Kings 8:12-13).

Since these three factors feed off each other and support each other, they are often found together. Readers of the Old Testament look back on the "glorious days of Solomon," recalling his wisdom, his wealth, and his spiritual judgment. Such a reading is very selective. 1 Kings 4:22-28 indicates that Solomon's great wealth and the vast amounts of food consumed by his court were paid for by taxes and contributions of the people. The picture sounds splended . . . for the king; it does not report the plight of the poor farmers who paid exorbitant taxes on their meager holdings to maintain Solomon's wealth. The question of fair distribution during Solomon's reign can hardly be addressed, since all distribution was directed toward meeting the needs of the king.

For such a system to work a certain kind of God was needed. This God lived in splended housing supplied by the king. This kind of God served as patron for the king and supported the total system. In such a system, giving to God and giving to the king were one and the same thing. When the poor called to God for help, their appeals were lost. Their requests were channeled through the royal priests, who themselves were wealthy and not about to upset a system which treated them so generously.

Issues related to food, justice, and freedom were heard, but immediately "put in their proper perspective;" the pressing concern was to maintain order and solidarity in the society. In this model, God was the head of a system where some worked little and ate much while others worked hard but ate little. Of course, God was not actually head of such an unjust system; but when the religious people insisted that he was, the innocent, uneducated lower classes, who had no way of knowing anything else, probably believed it to be true.

The Modern Myths of Solomon

We cannot repent of Solomon's oppressive system, but we can learn from it and wrestle with similar injustices in our own day. The three problems of Solomon's system are gradually becoming a way of life in our own world.

The repentance to which the problem of hunger calls the church is a repentance in three directions: (1) repentance of economic affluence which encourages acquisition and enjoyment of everything an individual wants, without considering its impact upon others; (2) repentance of political systems which support oppression by keeping hungry neighbors so far distant that no one thinks about them; (3) repentance of a religious system which has so totally domesticated God that he has become part of the system. Of course, God is not really part of this system, just as he was not in Solomon's day. Often, however, those in power try to get others to believe that God is standing with them and blessing their efforts to keep things as they are. God and religion still are used today much as they were used in Solomon's day—as a way for some to live well off the poverty of others.

Another aspect of hunger and affluence to examine is the issue of insufficient production. As noted earlier, growing more food will not entirely solve the problem. A program of sufficient production does not mean simply doubling the acreage in production. Probably that would not be possible. It is more important to look at what crops are being grown on the available acreage and to ask why they are being produced. Who benefits from those crops?

In the Bible, the questions of "nature," such as fertility, productivity, and land treatment are tied closely to the "historical-political" questions of justice and righteousness. Simply stated, when people are involved in doing justice together, the earth brings forth more abundantly. There is nothing magical about such a claim. The Bible suggests that productivity does not depend upon human knowledge of soils, seeds, and fertilizers: rather, productivity depends upon fidelity and covenant—the *desire* to do what is right rather than simply doing it because someone has the technical know-how.

Psalm 72, a royal psalm for the king, shows this fascinating interlocking of justice and fertility:

Give the king thy justice, O God,
    and thy righteousness to the royal son!
May he judge thy people with righteousness,
    and thy poor with justice!
Let the mountains bear prosperity for the people,
    and the hills, in righteousness!
May he defend the cause of the poor of the people,
    give deliverance to the needy,
    and crush the oppressor!
May he live while the sun endures,
    and as long as the moon, throughout all generations!
May he be like rain that falls on the mown grass,
    like showers that water the earth!
                           Psalm 72:1-6

Within the covenant community, famine, crop failure, and hunger are not separate from the covenant; they are deeply intertwined with the covenant. Society today, however, has become so accustomed to thinking in purely scientific or naturalistic terms that it is easy to forget the impact of God's word on these matters. Hear the voice of God in Leviticus 26:18-20: "If . . . you will not hearken to me, then I will chastize you again sevenfold for your sins, and I will break the pride of your power, and I will make your heavens like iron and your earth like brass; and your strength shall be spent in vain, for your land shall not yield its increase, and the trees of the land shall not yield their fruit."

How does doing justice affect the food supply? Hosea 4:1, 3 speaks to that issue: "For the Lord has a controversy with the inhabitants of the land. There is no faithfulness or kindness, and no knowledge of God in the land; . . . Therefore the land mourns, and all who dwell in it languish, and also the beasts of the field, and the birds of the air; and even the fish of the sea are taken away."

When God's basic law of living in harmony with creation is not obeyed, the land suffers; people fall out of relationship with the land and with each other. Thus both people and land are grossly misused. The produce of the land is redirected toward self-protection rather than toward producing basic foods which are needed for living. On a wider scale, rich nations use land which could grow food to sustain life for producing non-essential foods to satisfy the whims of western taste buds. Industrial nations no longer dare assume that people in other nations exist on subsistence wages, growing bananas, coffee, and tobacco, so that the rich and powerful might have the luxury of inexpensive, nonessential foods.

Such treatment of others, along with the demands made upon the land of others, indicates that there is no covenant relationship with them or with God. The whole earth is suffering for this. More fertilizer, more acreage, and better seed stock may help to alleviate some of the problem in a temporary way, but it is not the full solution. Such an approach is geared primarily at maintaining the present system which heavily favors the industrial nations of the West at the expense of poorer, developing nations.

A Call for Repentance

What is needed is a return to Godly covenant living which faces squarely the issues of freedom and justice. As

God's people rediscover the meaning of justice, they will also discover that God speaks to the issues of plenty and hunger. Then God's people may recognize that what God is saying demands repentance and new life from those who are claiming the name of Jesus.

The biblical message is clear. The issues of hunger and clothing are not secondary items for conferences to discuss; they are crucial items for the daily concern of each Christian and each congregation. James put it this way: "My brothers, what good is it for someone to say that he has faith if his actions do not prove it? Can that faith save him? Suppose there are brothers or sisters who need clothes and don't have enough to eat. What good is there in your saying to them, 'God bless you! Keep warm and eat well!'—if you don't give them the necessities of life?" (paraphrased)

A sign on the office door of a teaching colleague sums up the issue well: "All we ask is that you live simply so that others may simply live."

11.
Power and Oppression

John Woolman, an early American Quaker, once said, "May we look upon our treasures, the furniture of our houses, and our garments, and try to see whether the seeds of war have nourishment in these our possessions."

It may be hard to believe that the clothing, the furniture, the treasures of Christians could be the cause of injustice or oppression. Woolman's quote does, however, point to some basic questions which Christians must face. Just how big is our world? Who is included and who is excluded in our understanding of the world? What are the interrelationships of the people of the world?

What Is the Shape of the World?

In 1812 Elbridge Gerry, governor of Massachusetts, attempted to redivide the voting districts of his state in order to assure the election of certain persons from his own political party. As he carved up the local population to meet his own political goals, he created voting districts with extremely unusual shapes. One of his opponents objected, describing his efforts as producing something which resembled a "disjointed salamander." The term "gerrymander" was quickly applied to Governor Gerry's effort to create geographic groups of like-minded people.

Although Christians do not create such literal geographic areas, they are often guilty of "gerrymandering" in their social contacts. It is easy to weave in and out, around and among the people of the world, in order to be with people who are "like us" economically, socially, or culturally. By gerrymandering such friendships, people avoid contact with others who would challenge them to change their way of living. People thus associate most closely with those who affirm what they are doing and assure them that they are being good Christian people. All around these people, however, are other persons whose life experience is quite different. Their counsel, if it were heard, would be quite different and often much less assuring.

World political divisions are taking shape today less along the ideological lines of capitalism, socialism, and communism than along the lines of the haves and the have-nots, the powerful and the powerless, the oppressor and the oppressed. These new alignments are often unpleasant; they clutter up the neat categories that have become comfortable—WE, the capitalists or good guys, against THEM, the communists or the bad guys. More and more, however, other nations of the world are saying that both groups are equally at fault, for they both oppress weaker nations to get what they want for themselves.

A New Pax Romana?

Some Christian historians have drawn parallels between the Pax Romana of Jesus' day and the Pax Canada/U.S.A. of this age. Some common factors are seen in both ages: the oppressive relationship to other weaker nations; the primacy of a military force which is paid for by the people who are controlled by that force; the concern that those in control not be threatened by the people being controlled. In Jesus' day, Roman leaders tried to tell the world it was for their own good that Rome was in control. Jesus referred to this in Luke 22:25-27: "The kings of the gentiles exercise lordship over them; and those in authority over them are called benefactors. But not so with you; rather let the greatest among you become as the youngest, and the leader as one who serves."

Members of the powerful western nations are being told that their nations are supporting the development of the poorer nations; they are asked to believe that the West is truly being most generous with their resources. It is painful to have to face the fact that this is not the case. Ron Sider says that if we are members of a privileged group which benefits from a system that oppresses others and yet do nothing to try to change the way things are, then we stand guilty before God (*Christ & Violence,* Scottdale, Herald Press, 1979, p. 73).

Sider refers to the patterns of international trade as one example of power which oppresses other people. The nations of the industrial West have often shaped the patterns of trade for their own economic advantage. Tariff restrictions, import quotas, and other techniques are used to manipulate trade and control prices in favor of their own national manufacturers. Nations do not want their people buying less expensive products from poor countries when a similar product, made at home, is available for a higher price. They prefer to buy raw materials at low cost and keep the labor market costs at home rather than to have the poor country benefit from the manufacturing of the product before selling it to the rich nation. This attitude keeps rich people rich and poor people poor by denying the poor country the millions of jobs and billions of dollars they would realize in producing and exporting the finished product. In this way a rich country can control the people in a poor country; sadly, most of the people in the rich country are not even aware that this is happening.

A second major concern is the impact of eating habits upon the rest of the world. Rich nations have the power to control the prices of food which they import from poor nations. Food products are imported at low prices to feed animals. Much of this food could be used for human consumption in other countries; however, the price there is so high in comparison to the low wages paid the workers that people cannot afford to buy the food they are producing. For example, two thirds of the world's tuna fish is imported by the United States, and then one third of that amount is fed to cats.

Power and oppression have a way of going hand in hand, although most people often do not recognize this. People living in the powerful nations are not evil and vindictive, intentionally making life hard for others. Usually they simply are not aware of how their actions affect others. Sometimes their concern to keep things as they are so completely dominates their lives that they are unable to think in other ways. Many people participate in evil by proxy, simply by assuming that the way they live is about average and that there is no need for change. It is difficult for these persons to comprehend that Jesus is talking to them about the gospel of a new way and a new life.

The Distortion of History

On the local scene power and oppression is felt in yet another way. Frequently, history changes the way people look at things. Within our own religious tradition, we recall with admiration certain things done by people many years ago. We admire them for their courage and faith. We refer to them as heroic examples for our children to follow. Yet when our children take steps of faith which are slightly different, though equally courageous, we are less enthusiastic and sometimes even openly critical.

There are many stories of persons who took a stand for their faith and went to jail for that stand. Martin Luther King and many others were imprisoned during the struggle for racial equality in the United States. Bob Gross, a Church of the Brethren youth from Indiana, served an eighteen-month sentence in a federal penitentiary for his refusal to cooperate with the draft system. In our religious tradition and history, we know of many other such stories. Yet we also know of our society's myth which says that people are in prison because they are criminals; after all, if they were not criminals, why would they be in jail? The experience of our religious heritage, however, says strongly that this is not always the case. Sometimes persons are in jail because they are being obedient to Jesus Christ.

Then why are we conservative Christians so willing to accept this popular myth today? Why are persons so quick to be critical of our own young people who, because of deep religious conviction, stand in opposition to the demands of the culture upon their lives, who say "no" to a monstrous military presence, who face the threat of being sent to prison for their desire to be faithful to Jesus? Why are these young people not seen as modern heroes of the faith just as their ancestors are upheld as faith heroes? Admittedly, in a few cases they are supported and encouraged; most frequently, however, the tendency is to feel that somehow they are wrong, that they are compromising their faith, that they are being poor witnesses to Jesus and the Christian faith.

When this happens, the world and not the kingdom of God is shaping the patterns of thought and life for the Christian. The assumptions of the world become the basic assumptions for the Christian as well. This acceptance of the world's assumptions leads Christians to an increasing support of a system which is oppressive, dehumanizing, and in basic conflict with the kingdom of God.

Does Forgiving Mean Punishing?

When Jesus announced the presence of the kingdom of God in his sermon at Nazareth, one aspect of that presence was that prisoners would be released. Often when this is mentioned, respectable middle-class persons sense a minor panic; they visualize emptying the jails and turning dangerous persons loose on the streets; they fear that communities will no longer be safe. This reaction is an example of the irrational responses people often make when they do not fully understand a situation. Rather than wrestling seriously with the life and teachings of Jesus in order to determine what to do, they quickly take an extreme position based on fear and social propaganda.

Christians from the peace churches have long wrestled with the question of war as the way to handle disputes. They have decided that war is unacceptable as a means for handling disputes, even though much of society feels differently about the solutions they suggest. Perhaps it is also time for the peace churches to consider a new approach to prisons, punishment, and rehabilitation. Even as members of the peace churches have challenged society's assumptions about war, perhaps they can now challenge the assumptions about life in other areas as well.

Most Christians have given very little thought to the issues of crime, punishment, and rehabilitation. Crime and prisoners are approached by many Christians in ways that are almost identical to everyone else's approach. People who do wrong should be punished, and that punishment should be sufficiently severe to discourage the person or anyone else from repeating the crime.

Prisons are built on the assumption that some persons deserve to suffer. The popular sentiment of "he had it coming to him" is built on the belief that when persons do something wrong they have to pay for it. This approach is not found in the teachings of Jesus. When persons did what was wrong, Jesus called them to repentance. Those who were sinned against were not told to punish, but rather to forgive and restore the wrongdoer to wholeness.

It is common to go back to the Old Testament and apply what is called by some "the law of retaliation" (*lex talionis*) to crime. This law calls for "an eye for an eye . . . a tooth for a tooth . . . a life for a life" (Exod. 21:24). At that time the Israelites understood this as God's command for justice: do unto others what others have done unto you. The redemption of the offending person back into being a constructive, responsible member of society was seldom mentioned.

Recently a prominent spokesperson in American life said with some vehemence that all people involved in drug traffic should be jailed for life and the key thrown away. Is it possible, however, to ardently oppose all forms of drug traffic and do everything possible to stop it, and yet see the drug dealer as a person who needs redemption and redirection for his or her life? Is the only option for dealing with those who traffic in drugs to throw them in jail? Have we decided that repentance and salvation is beyond the grasp of, or even too good for, some persons?

Is There a Word From the Scriptures?

The quick application of the Old Testament law of retaliation is an excellent example of misusing a biblical concept to support the current penal practice. This is a gross misunderstanding of the concept. It was not a divine command on how to treat persons who did something wrong. In fact, it was almost the opposite. The purpose of this law was to restrict the use of retaliation which was so common in that culture—to avoid the escalating spiral of violence. Rather than requiring and demanding any eye for an eye, it limited punishment to not more than an eye for an eye. The purpose was to keep a sense of proportion between the crime and the punishment.

A second problem in using this Old Testament law of retaliation as a way of viewing punishment is that it tends to see God as one who punishes for the sake of vengeance. While such an approach expresses the human desire for vengeance, it overlooks the fact that the purpose of God's judgment and punishment was not to cause an equal amount of suffering but to turn the Israelites from their sinful ways and lead them back to a path of rightousness. Ezekiel expressed this concern: "As I live, says the Lord, I swear I take no pleasure in the death of a wicked man, but rather in the wicked man's conversion, and that he may live. Turn, turn from your evil ways! Why should you die, O house of Israel?" (Ezek. 33:11 paraphrased)

This same spirit is found in the words of Jesus as he talks about this Old Testament concept of retaliation. Jesus repudiated the concept when he said: "You have heard that it was said, 'An eye for an eye, and a tooth for a tooth.' But now I tell you, do not take revenge on someone who does you wrong" (Matt. 5:38-39 paraphrased)

Jesus called for and exhibited an ethic of love in place of vengeance and retribution. As part of this ethic, Jesus rejected the condemnation of others: "Do not judge others and God will not judge you; do not condemn others and God will not condemn you; forgive others and God will forgive you" (Luke 6:37 paraphrased)

This same theme of the kingdom approach to punishment is also found in Paul's writings: "If someone does evil to you, do not pay him back with evil. Try to do what all men consider to be good. Do everything possible on your part to live at peace with all men. Never take revenge, my friends, but instead let God's wrath do it . . . Instead, as the Scripture says: 'If he is thirsty, give him a drink; for by doing this you will heap burning coals of fire on his head.' Do not let evil defeat you; instead conquer evil with good" (Rom. 12:17-21 paraphrased).

Is There a Better Way?

What then should be done with the criminal? How can a

safe society be maintained? As long as Christians continue accepting the assumptions of the world about who criminals are and what should be done with them, not much progress will be made. Perhaps a simple comparison of the Old Testament procedure with current practices will help our understanding.

In the Old Testament if fraud was discovered after a sale, the product was returned to the seller and a penalty of 20 percent was required (Lev. 27:13, 27). If something was stolen, it was to be returned and a penalty of 20 percent was exacted from the thief (Lev. 6:5-6). Leviticus 22:4 also calls for a 100 percent penalty in certain cases. There was a set schedule for repayment in cases where something was stolen, then lost, sold, or destroyed so that it could not be returned (five oxen returned for one oxen stolen; four sheep returned for one sheep stolen, etc.) If the person had no property, he himself was to be sold into slavery—a primitive form of garnisheeing wages—to pay the debt (Exod. 22:3). In cases of personal injury, the person inflicting the injury was required to pay all wages which were lost while the injured person recuperated (Exod. 21:18-19).

The current system operates quite differently. If something is stolen, the person responsible is put in jail to await trial. If the person is poor and cannot afford bail, this waiting period frequently runs from two to six months. Because such a person has not yet been proven guilty, he or she is still innocent according to the law, but is kept in jail anyway. During this time the person often loses a job and the income needed to support a family; at the same time, the local community pays the high cost of maintaining a person in prison. The circle of pain and hardship thus goes far beyond the thief and the victim.

Little attempt is made to bring the person and the victim together for possible reconciliation. In fact, most of the energy is spent in keeping the two persons far apart. Other people are hired to confront the accused person; these confronters (lawyers) are paid high wages to do what Christians themselves should do in basic love and humility.

Reconciliation is not part of the penal language; what is emphasized is punishment for the crime. And what happens? The victim pays higher insurance premiums because

Nguyen Van Gia

of the claim filed to replace the stolen property. Taxes go up to pay for supporting the prison system. The criminal, who was probably struggling with adjustment problems in life already, has the added pressure of family disruption and community stigma. Even worse, this stigma often carries over to the children, though they are in no way responsible for what has happened. Frequently the state needs to give financial aid to the family through the welfare system or other social programs. Thus, all persons in the community, not just those directly involved, suffer.

Isn't there a better way? Members of the kingdom of God should be saying "yes" to this question. But exactly how should they be saying yes? How can the followers of Jesus bring a new vision of justice to a world that is playing the power and punishment game with the lives of people?

Present-day justice seems to have one goal in mind: find someone who has done wrong and mete out punishment. Little care is shown for the criminal's needs or the victim's loss. The justice which Jesus advocated would attempt to restore both the criminal and the victim to a relationship which recognizes the full humanity of each; thus, the whole community could live together in peace and dignity.

While society focuses on punishment, the Bible first calls for Christians to give attention to repairing both the immediate injustice of the crime itself and the background injustices which led to the crime. A quick sense of outrage may tempt Christians to follow society's model; that model, however, has been highly ineffective. In fact, society's model for dealing with criminals usually contributes to the problem rather than solving it.

Second, whether the offender is a petty thief, a frantic person looking for a quick way out of an immediate crisis, or a corporation official embezzling funds, such a person needs to be confronted with his actions. Society focuses on the quick removal of the person from the community. Christians ought to focus on the rehabilitation of the offender back into the community. The problem is not solved by imposing a stiff punishment on the offender. Nor is it solved by acting as though what happened does not matter; indeed it does matter. Rather, both reconciliation and restitution are needed; reconciliation and restitution thus become the key to a new kingdom model.

How Does it Work?

At various places in the world persons are working hard at models of Christian reconciliation. Probably the most famous is the work of Chuck Colson's Prison Fellowship. As the result of his own experience in prison, Colson has committed his life as an active Christian to prison visitation and reform and prisoner rehabilitation. His monthly newsletter, "Jubilee," attempts to share this new vision with other believers. Colson insists that it is not enough to keep people out of the system, for that is unrealistic. Christians must also work for drastic reform so that persons caught in the system can be set free to find a new life.

Another attempt at living the Jesus approach to prisoners is the Victim Offender Reconciliation Program (VORP) of Kitchener, Ontario and Elkhart, Indiana. Whenever possible, the offender and the victim are brought together and a process of restitution agreeable to both parties is negotiated. Rather than focusing on jail and punishment, the focus is upon reconciliation and restitution. Another aspect of VORP allows a judge, in cases of minor felony or misdemeanor, to assign a person to a supervised, non-paying community work program at the rate of six hours a day for every day required by the normal jail sentence. Such jobs are provided by churches, community organizations, and the county. It is estimated that this program saves more than $36.00 a day per person for the state. On several occasions, persons serving this free work-time sentence have become so involved in the work that they continued to volunteer time even after the sentence was served.

Called to Express a New Way

Many voices within the culture and the government still insist that the only way to handle crime is by harsh punishment. If the price of misbehaving is high enough, then people will be good. However, studies of this approach have shown time after time that this philosophy does not work. Similarly, many voices in the culture say that individuals and groups can do little to change global practices which oppress the powerless. Yet, we continue to see new evidence that current practices are not working well for the total world community. Thus, it is time for the church to give expression to a new approach to justice issues.

Various programs of ministry with prisoners are offering guidance to a rethinking of some of our culture's fundamental assumptions about criminal justice. New understandings of the relatedness of the nations of the world are making people aware of oppression on a global scale. New ways of confronting these expressions of power and oppression in our society and in our world are being discovered. The kingdom of God does bring hope to those who are in prison, to the powerless, to the oppressed.

The call of Christ is for Christians to proclaim the message of a new way; this includes a new way of becoming involved with those whom the world rejects, whom the world tries to hide from view as being valueless or dangerous. Jesus said: "The Spirit of the Lord is upon me . . . . He has sent me to proclaim release to the captives . . . . "

Is the church hearing the message of Jesus?

12.
The Kingdom of Heaven and the Kingdom of Earth

If you could ask several Christians living in the fourth century what they thought about the problem of church and state, they probably would reply, "What problem are you talking about? We used to have a problem, but we don't anymore because the emperor is now a Christian. In fact we will most likely never have a church-state problem again, and for this we praise God."

Things had changed for Christians in the fourth century. The years of anxiety and persecution were over. The prayers of the martyrs had been heard and God had liberated the people once more. With the conversion of the emperor Constantine with all his military and political power, the church was assured an era of peace and blessing.

Similarly, some persons today believe that the way to peace in the world is to get devout Christian people into the seats of power. The state could then enforce the morality of the church and the gospel would flourish once again. The call is for the salvation of the rulers with the unspoken assumption being that if you get the king you will also get all the king's court.

For more than a thousand years after Constantine, the church functioned as the spiritual counterpart to the political organization of the state. The church was so organized that it exercised power in much the same way as the state exercised power. The church and state lived together almost like identical twins. While there were arguments over who controlled what, underneath such arguments was the basic agreement that church and state belonged together.

One of the issues in the Reformation was the place of the state in the life of the church. How much authority should it have over the church? What happens when the state wants something which conflicts with what the church believes is right? In the minds of some people such a conflict would not be possible since both the church and the state are ordained by God. Thus the mainstream Reformation group (Luther, Zwingli, Calvin) carefully negotiated with the state at each step of the way. The more radical wing of the Reformation (Grebel, Manz, Blaurock), however, focused on what they felt was right for the church without asking permission from the state. Therefore, it is not surprising that conflict developed between these radical reformers and the state, as well as between the radicals and other reformers.

God's Primary Concern is the Church

In the early days of its existence, the church quickly became a threat to the Roman empire. The church challenged the idea that the state was the incarnation of divine authority. Though the early Christians were a peaceful group of followers, they were convinced that the state was not an all-powerful organization which carried the divine sanction of God for all it wanted to do. Far too often throughout history, Christians have lost this profound concept and accepted the state's convincing arguments that it should have unqualified and almost reverent obedience.

The Christian church needs to return to the foundational assumption that the primary focus of God is upon his people, the church. A return to this focus would help Christians avoid the idolatry of worshiping the state and its attempts to issue ultimate commands.

The church, not the state, is God's primary concern. The church is the agent of God's redemption in history. The state is simply a politically expedient organization which assists people in ordering their lives while they live together

Three Lions

in a certain geographic area. Thus, while the state continues to live by the permissive will of God, the center stage of history, in God's eyes at least, has been given over to the people of God. Through the church God will complete his reconciling work begun in Jesus Christ. In the body of Christ all things will eventually be united in Christ Jesus.

The meaning of history, when told by the secular historian, is frequently given in terms of battles and governments and treaties between nations. For the believer, the meaning of history is found in the redemptive work of Jesus Christ and in the redemptive community of his people. These people live within the boundaries of the state, but they recognize that the state is not on the same level as the church. The state serves the function of restraining the evildoer and refereeing the selfishness and violence which goes on in this sinful world. Never, however, dare the church relinquish the ultimate authority of God to such a temporary organization as the national state.

The Church as an Alternative to the State

One perspective for understanding the issue of church and state is to see the church as an alternative to the state. This viewpoint holds that the greatest witness the church can make is to be faithful to its calling to be the church. The church should be a counter-community over against the state, a visible expression of God's way of doing things, an example of peace and biblical shalom in the midst of a world intent upon war, destruction, and the separation of people. The church should be a community of faith that dares to give expression to what it believes God has revealed, a community that fulfills the words of Jesus when he called his followers to be light and salt to the world. Paul had this kind of community in mind when he wrote to the Philippians about being a "colony of heaven," being a people of peace who incarnate justice and love.

Thus the most prophetic calling which the church can undertake is simply to be the church. But it often seems so much more exciting to take on the world and play the game of power politics along with the nations of the world. This is one temptation the church always has to face.

In our Anabaptist tradition, most of us live in relative

comfort in a local community; often the issue of church-state does not seem very critical. We are not involved in playing the political game. Usually we are respected and trusted in business and community participation. Sometimes we wonder how to best participate in the local community government. What offices can or should we hold? Where or how should we take a stand, saying either "yes" or "no" to certain issues? There are significant differences among members of our congregations about how we should confront these situations.

Some persons have defined the kingdom of heaven in a way that emphasizes the fundamental differences between this kingdom and the state; this understanding makes participation in either state or local government virtually impossible. During much of our Anabaptist background, the state was directly involved in harsh persecution; consequently, our ancestors were not quick to give the state much credit as an agent of God. The notion developed that the more authentic and true the people of God were, the less involved they would be with the state.

This idea has led us at times to overlook those areas where the concerns and activities of the state overlap with the basic concerns of the church. We have felt more comfortable being critical of the state than cooperating with it. Yet in many areas we have cooperated a great deal. These decisions about where to cooperate and where not to cooperate have often caused confusion for us.

Society often thinks in extremes and the church can easily get caught in this same tendency. If we cooperate at one level, such as working in the post office or serving on the city zoning board, we are challenged to be consistent and participate in every area of government. On the other hand, if we object to participation in one area, such as war, there are those who think it would be consistent to leave the country since we obviously object to all areas of national life. But should these extreme positions guide us? Should not the Christian be able to discriminate as to where and how personal resources and time are to be used?

The State as God's System in the World

A second perspective for understanding the church-state question is to see the state as God's system in the world. During the Reformation, radical leaders insisted that the states received from God their authority for the restraining of evil and the rewarding of good. Precise limits were placed on what the state could do. National boundaries were seen as a human division intended to separate people into opposing groups or factions. Since the radical leaders saw themselves as subjects of God, who was Lord over all people, they felt free to disregard the claims of absolute authority made by national rulers.

But that position has not always been kept very clear. Anabaptists today have discovered that they do not live alone in the world. Other people, who are also part of the Christian community, hold different points of view on this question. They place fewer limitations on the state, believing that the state can be God's way of order in the world. In the broad Anabaptist tradition, however, persons have held that refusal to participate in the life of the state was essential in their obedience to God; especially was this true when the state called people to take up arms to protect the state against its enemies. Other Christian people, however, have differed with the Anabaptists on this point.

A Witness and Yet Separate

The viewpoint which sees the state as God's system in the world has some appeal for our peace-loving traditions, especially since life in Canada and the United States has generally brought wealth and security to most of our churches. This has led some of our members to listen rather closely when Christian friends argue that it is simply responsible citizenship before God to defend the good life we have come to enjoy.

Perhaps Brethren in Christ, Mennonite, and Church of the Brethren congregations should be honest and admit that it is not so much a pure theological concern for the state which most of our members feel when they talk about national defense. Perhaps it is more realistic to recognize that the basic desire is to protect the wealth and privilege which has been granted by the nation.

In light of biblical faith, it seems clear that the state has some authority and power right now. But the Christian community has a longer vision than the simple reality of "right now." The true church does appear weak and, at times, ineffective and even despised as it cries out for justice and love. Yet the church's faith is in God who rules now and forever; in the final view, the state will be judged by God.

Thus it is appropriate for the church to talk about witness to the state and yet remain separate from the state. Paul used this approach (Acts 24) as he debated with Felix about justice and judgment. This approach does not depend on threats or ultimatums; the intention is not to take over the controls and run government more effectively. Rather, the church is called to operate out of a stance of deep integrity, speaking out for the poor because the church itself is deeply involved in ministry to the poor; asking for social and racial justice because the church has already been sharing, integrating, and giving to those in need. Unfortunately, too many churches are still influenced by the values of the kingdom of this earth, not the values of the kingdom of heaven. Therefore, the church's witness is often seen as self-serving or inconsistent, trying to protect itself rather than giving of itself for others.

The Church's Witness to the State

Does all this mean that Christians should not participate in government in any way? Such a question cannot be answered with a simple "yes" or "no". The Bible does offer some helpful counsel for considering the issue.

Peter tells believers to "submit for the Lord's sake" (1 Pet. 2:13-17). Some persons interpret this to mean that Christians should do whatever the state asks, with no questions raised. In such a setting it is crucial for believers to back up one step and reaffirm that they are first of all members of the kingdom of God. All commands for obedience from any other organization must be screened through this primary commitment. Jesus, not the state, is Lord. Once in a while the state forgets that and tries to act as though it is Lord over Christians. When the state so acts, Christians need to carefully and prayerfully discern the will of God before acting.

Christians are indeed citizens of an earthly nation and are not exempt from the laws of those nations; however, to consider God and the national order as equals is a gross misreading of the Scripture. The constant danger is that Christians will turn over to the state the responsibility of discerning truth and allow the state to dictate what "Christian behavior" will look like.

Peter's words in 1 Peter 2:13-17 imply that Christians will not need the state because all Christians live upright lives and do not cause any trouble. The text also assumes that the state will behave in an upright and moral way, doing what God intended the state to do. The real difficulty comes when the state pursues its own interests and then tries to pass those off as God's will.

In all this, the behavior of Christians should be such a striking witness that it precludes criticism or argument. For when obedience to God is unclear, it is easy to give mixed signals to the state about what obedience means. When such unclarity exists, the result is justified confusion and criticism from the state and from other Christians.

How Then Shall We Act?

Persons can take one of various positions with regard to political involvement. Sincere Christians are found at each position, convinced that theirs is the right path of obedience to Christ. One stance is a purist position which refuses any form of organized participation. Persons adhering to this stance see the two kingdoms—the kingdom of this world and the kingdom of God—so far apart that the only solution is to stand outside the political system, ignoring it as much as possible. On rare occasion these persons will speak a word of constructive criticism to the state. Normally, however, they see the kingdom of God as a radical alternative to the political systems of this world.

A second stance is actually several different stances all lumped together; it involves limited participation with the line being drawn at many different places. Persons operating from this position look at what is happening in a given situation and decide whether it is possible to be part of the political organization at this particular level. Some persons will serve as appointed members of local city or county committees. Others choose to run for elected office on the local level. Still others join in the state government process but stop short of national office because of military budget implications for their peace stance. Other persons will vote in elections but not serve in political office themselves.

The third stance is full participation. Persons who operate out of this stance believe that Christians should work within the structure of government on every level in order to see that wisdom and compassion are expressed throughout the total system.

Which stance is the proper one? Though one person cannot answer that question for all Christians, perhaps some counsel will assist in the decision-making process. Behind these words of counsel is the assumption that this decision will be made with the counsel of the community of faith, not in isolation. *What Have You To do With Peace* by Walter Klaassen (Altona, Manitoba. D. W. Friesen and Sons, Ltd., 1969) provides the foundation for the following comments.

Total non-involvement in the political world is extremely hard to comprehend. Simply by living within the geographic boundaries of the system, persons paricipate to some degree in what the government does. Even by their silence, people participate! How often someone in office has claimed to be representing the "silent majority."

On the other extreme, the state can easily expect and ask for ultimate allegiance. The state may try to convince its citizens that it is supreme, that its continued existence is the most important thing on earth. This is idolatry and needs to be seen as such. When a nation calls upon its citizens to go to war to defend the state, it assumes that people are a product which can be consumed in order to achieve the current national goal. This means that people are called upon to die for something which is of lesser value than they are. Is it possible for Christians to be so completely involved in a political system that they will advocate the sacrifice of human beings for the protection of the state?

Between these two extremes, however, lie some other options.

1. Christians can pray regularly for those in authority (1 Tim. 2:2). Leaders need prayer so that they might have wisdom and compassion in ruling. They are bombarded daily by persons who are convinced that God is on the side of

this issue or that project. Much wisdom is needed to sort out truth from greedy human desire.

2. Christians should be grateful for the order which national governments bring to civic life. In spite of the jokes and complaints, the mail does get through, roads are maintained, drugs and medicines are tested for safety and effectiveness. Though those in authority do not always decide issues the way some people would wish, the overwhelming majority of leaders want to restrain evil and promote good as they understand it.

3. Christians need to recognize the role of government in providing a wide variety of services to citizens. These include social security, pensions for the aged, education scholarships, unemployment insurance, welfare assistance, and research in mental health, cancer, and retardation. Most Christians can enthusiastically support these projects because they are founded on generally constructive principles, seeking the good of all people.

4. Christians, in both Canada and the United States, should appreciate that their government is representative, intended to reflect the will of the people. Christians need to be in conversation with government, sharing words of commendation when the state fulfills its God-given function. Christians also have the responsibility to give counsel when the state fails to do what it should do. Such failure can be either neglecting to do good or doing that which is destructive. In both cases, the church should be alert to injustice and speak to government on behalf of those persons to whom justice is due.

5. Christians need to think carefully about those current Christian organizations which insist that the only hope for the nation is to "Christianize" the government, by electing to public office only people with certain religious convictions. Such organizations assume that all "true Christians" will have identical Christian convictions.

Senator Mark Hatfield urges Christians to be cautious of such groups, to remember the Holy Roman Empire when Christians could not distinguish between the banner of commitment to Christ and the flag of obedience to the state. Hatfield recalls that it was out of this supposedly divine merger that the Crusades developed, with their brutality conducted in the name of Jesus. Such merger also called forth mass conversions, under the threat of the sword, and the Inquisition, which controlled doctrine through the use of torture. Many of these same themes are being resurrected today by persons who are trying to bring church and state together: an ever-increasing military budget for national defense (preparation for a modern crusade against pagan infidels in other nations?); restrictions on office holders, appointing only those of correct theological persuasion to influential government posts; withholding tax benefits from organizations which are critical of the government.

It is easy to be confused by such movements for bringing together church and state, for the 10 percent of their iceberg which is above the surface sounds very correct to our religious ears. Unfortunately, though, the submerged 90 percent holds a frightening combination of political power, military might, and economic favoritism through privileges given to a few. All of this is wrapped in a cloak of religious language which appeals to many sincere Christians.

6. Christians carry a basic responsibility to be informed on the issues of life. Every organization has its own system for gathering information and dispensing what it believes to be the "truth." Government is no different. One crucial service which the church can give to government is to supply facts which otherwise would be rejected by the internal information-gathering system. The people are told that government knows best because they know more. That is a myth. Much information which government officials receive comes through the single window of a military orientation to problem solving; this reflects a strong bias which the church should endeavor to correct.

7. Christians should also remember that they are a people in mission for others. If Christians contact government only to get or to protect special interests for themselves, they are not being faithful. While it is important to inform legislators how certain proposed laws would affect the church, self-protection should be secondary to mission for those who have no voice.

The church must also be aware of the high cost of

privilege. Persons who benefit from the concessions which the government grants frequently find it difficult to speak a word of challenge to government; they are afraid these privileges will be withdrawn. Canadians are very cautious about being too anxious to help American draft resisters for fear of losing their own conscientious objector status. Americans are urging each other to be careful in speaking to the government about war or war taxes, fearing their conscientious objector status will be withdrawn. The nation knows this as well and has, in time of war, tried to buy the silence of the peace churches by granting such exemptions, hoping that then the churches will not get in the way of the national war effort. Silence is a valuable commodity for government, and granting special privileges is one way of buying silence.

First Allegiance

The political orders of our day still try to convince us that they are doing God's will for the nation and that Christians within the peace church tradition should unquestioningly join with them in whatever they want to do. The challenge to the church is to remember that there are two kingdoms, and while they do on occasion overlap, they are not one and the same. The determining factor for the church should always be its primary commitment to Jesus Christ as Lord. All other agenda must be placed under that first allegiance. If the activity of the state overlaps with what the church understands its own agenda to be, then some participation might be possible. But the church must never abdicate the responsibility of discernment, must never allow the state to determine the meaning of faithfulness. Jesus is Lord, and that cry must remain the church's statement of faith.

13.
Thy Kingdom Come

The apostle Peter, explaining the events of Pentecost to the Jewish people in Jerusalem (Acts 2:17), referred to the prophet Joel:
And in the last days it shall be, God declares,
that I will pour out my Spirit upon all flesh,
and your sons and your daughters shall prophesy,
and your young men shall see visions,
and your old men shall dream dreams; . . .

Dreaming dreams and seeing visions is an important part of life. Without dreams and visions of the future, life stays pretty much the way it is. Those people with the ability and insight to dream about how things could be help others to discover new things. However, the fine line between dreaming dreams and just being a dreamer is frequently difficult to maintain. One person dreams about the future and then acts upon the present to make that future a reality. Another person simply dreams, does nothing about it, and nothing changes.

To live in the present, persons desperately need some sense of vision for the future. For the Christian, that vision includes the confidence that God is in charge and that the future is not a frightening event; it is, rather, an exciting hope based on the assurance of God's love.

Dreaming about the future, however, can clash with the

necessity of living in the present. This clash is felt within the life of the church when some persons focus their faith upon a home in heaven while others say that the real point of the gospel is helping homeless people find houses in this world. Where should the focus of the church be? Do Christians decide that this world is an unredeemable mess and therefore spend their energies planning for the future? Or is this present life all there is, so that believers should do all they can to make it meaningful?

When faced with such differences in Christian understanding, it is far too easy to polarize and become rigid in one position or the other. The above questions cannot be answered with a simple "yes" or "no," for neither answer is totally correct, and both are dismally incomplete by themselves. The greatest danger is when the two get separated from each other; then Christians begin to believe that the half answer is the full answer and that all other answers are categorically wrong. When this happens, the creative tension between the presence of the kingdom of God and the fullness of the kingdom which is yet to come is lost. The loss of such tension cuts God's history into pieces, with each piece of history following the preceding one; in reality, however, the coming of Jesus Christ brings a great deal of overlapping of the present age with the coming kingdom.

The Bible describes the kingdom as an emerging reality which is here now, though far from complete in its present form. Christians do not bring the kingdom into reality, nor do they make it happen; it is the power of God which brings the kingdom. The believer can only bear witness to its truth and presence and live in obedience to the teachings of Jesus who is Lord of that kingdom. This kingdom is growing and expanding, and through the witness of believers it becomes visible to others. At times people see and believe; at other times people see, say "no" to the claims of Christ, and continue living in the old kingdoms of this world.

When Is the End Coming?

History seems to have a certain rhythm about it. Interest in the coming kingdom fluctuates, based on a number of economic and social issues. In recent years, as western nations have dealt more responsibly with their patterns of living and have recognized the influence of other nations upon their lives, many people have been tempted to turn outside of history, looking for God to provide a dramatic solution to the problem. One possible solution is that very soon God will set up a new kingdom in heaven and Christians will be delivered from the awful mess in this world. When people feel threatened and afraid, there is a general movement toward an expectation of the end of time. People want to escape from the pressures of the moment into the perfect bliss of God's eternal kingdom.

In 1741, Jonathan Edwards, a Puritan preacher in New England preached a sermon that has become well known in religious circles. In "Sinners in the Hands of an Angry God," Edwards described God as holding the sinner over the pit of hell much as one holds a spider or other loathsome insect over the fire, seeing human beings as worthy of nothing else but to be cast into the fires of hell and destruction. So vivid and forceful was Edwards' delivery that some of the audience actually grabbed hold of the tent posts and lashing ropes in the fear that their feet would slip and they would be plunged into everlasting damnation.

In that period, much attention was given to the end of time and all the various things which were thought to go with the end. In our day, people are again caught up in similar concerns. Persons are warned to get ready for this impending event while there is still time. Fear and other pressures are used to persuade persons to respond to Jesus now, thus misusing or missing completely the hope which was so central in Jesus' message about the kingdom of God.

The Meaning of History

If the kingdom of God is here as Jesus said it was, then what are we waiting for? What should we be doing while we are waiting?

In order to answer these questions, another question must be asked first. Though it sounds like a hard question, in reality it is not so bad: "What is the meaning of history?"

The Greeks have had a profound influence upon the way people think. They believed that history goes in circles and simply repeats itself; civilizations come and go, nations rise and fall, and other nations rise up in their place. The Greeks used the life cycle of a flower to illustrate what they meant: a flower grows in the spring, blooms throughout the summer, fades in the autumn, and dies in winter only to repeat the cycle again the following year.

The Hebrew people of the Old Testament had a different understanding of history. They believed that history was linear—that it was going somewhere, that it had a beginning and an ending. While the Greeks believed that God or the gods operated outside of history in a special realm, the Hebrews believed that God was involved in the beginning of history, that God operated within history (although not limited by it), and that God would be involved in the end of history.

What does all this mean? How does this help our understanding of the overlapping of the present and future aspects of the kingdom? Further examples and several diagrams may help.

Hebrew thought in the Old Testament saw history in three separate periods, periods which were separated by two great events: *Creation* and *The Day of The Lord* (Zeph. 1:7-18; Amos 5:18; Micah 2:4; 4:6). Time exists only during the period between *Creation* and *The Day*. Eternity is the period which comes after *The Day*. In eternity, time has no relevance—a day is as a thousand years. The following diagram illustrates this concept:

```
                        Creation           The Day of the Lord
                           |                       |
(Before Creation)          |       (Time)          |      (Eternity)
                           |                       |
```

For the Christian, this understanding of history is inadequate because it does not include the coming of Jesus into the world. Jesus' coming makes some significant changes in how history is now understood.

Jesus came announcing the presence of the kingdom, which Jewish people believed would come as part of *The Day of the Lord* and would go on forever, into eternity. But suddenly, all things were affected by the presence of Jesus and his announcement of the kingdom. The end faded in its dramatic significance, and the present aspect of the kingdom of God became central. The end had not been eliminated, but its impact was substantially affected by the coming of Jesus into the world.

Thus, the followers of Jesus live in a period of tension. They still live within time, affected by the demands of the earthly nations, but they also live under the lordship of Christ. It is understandable why so many Christians get their identities confused. The kingdom has come, but it is not yet complete; this forces Christians to live with a "here but not here" tension until the kingdom comes in its fullness.

The coming of Jesus changes the diagram of history so that it now looks like this:

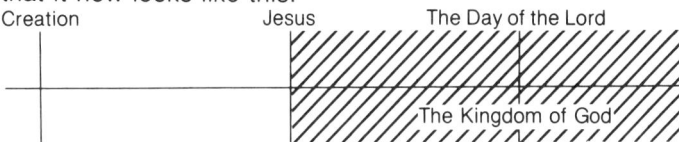

```
Creation              Jesus         The Day of the Lord
                      ////////////////////////////
──────────────────────////////////////////////////
                      //////The Kingdom of God////
                      ////////////////////////////
```

We are now living in the shaded area between the advent of the kingdom in Jesus and the Day of the Lord when the kingdom of God is experienced in its completeness.

The Joy of Our Present Security in Christ

This understanding of history which sees the present and future aspects of the kingdom overlapping helps to give meaning to some confusing terminology of our day. For example, eternal life is often presented as something which is received either after death or when *The Day* comes. But since Jesus has come and *The Day* has not yet come, apparently eternal life is not being withheld for the future; in fact, it has burst in upon us in the present age. The Christian shares in eternal life right now through a living faith in Jesus Christ who is Lord of this kingdom which has come. Becoming members of the kingdom of God now removes the anxiety about the future, because the coming of *The Day* or the coming of death, whichever is first, will have no effect whatever upon our relationship to God. Thus the words of Paul take on vivid meaning: "O death, where is thy victory? O death, where is thy sting? . . . Thanks be to God, who gives us the victory through Jesus Christ our Lord" (1 Cor. 15:55, 57).

Paul picks up this theme again in 2 Corinthians 6:2 as

he strongly affirms the presence of the kingdom and its meaning for salvation: "Behold, now is the accepted time; behold, now is the day of salvation." This verse has often been used to pressure people into making decisions for Christ immediately, before it is too late. That is exactly the opposite of what Paul had in mind. He is saying that the day of salvation has burst in upon us in Christ: it is no longer simply a future hope; it has in Christ become a present reality. We do not have to wait for God's future intervention into history; we can join God's kingdom movement right now and our salvation is assured.

What profound meaning this brings to Christians as they contemplate life, salvation, and the kingdom of God. While much of western preaching, and almost all of American and Canadian television preaching, talks a lot about Jesus, it does not deal seriously enough with the reality of his life and the presence of the kingdom here and now. Television preachers often proclaim that Jesus promises future blessings and calls believers to a future salvation in heaven. People are assured that when *The Day* comes they will receive the salvation which they now hope for by faith. This message is at best incomplete. The teachings of Jesus are filled with active verbs which describe what is to be experienced right now in this life.

For what are Christians waiting? Certainly for the culmination of their faith: however, that is not simply the anticipation of a future salvation, for the kingdom of God has come in Jesus. Christians wait for the final completion or perfection of that which they already are experiencing as members of the kingdom of God.

What Do We Do Now?

The second question is a logical outgrowth of the first: "What should we be doing while we wait for the completion of our salvation?" Robert Friedmann has written an interesting study, *The Theology of Anabaptism* (Scottdale, Herald Press, 1973). In this book he notes the great attention given to the return of Jesus in the 1500s. Almost every religious group lived in anticipation of this great event. Friedmann says that while the radical reformers shared this belief about the return of the Lord, their approach to it was quite different. They emphasized the impact of the future upon them right now; they lived in God's presence, even in their adversity, rather than joining those who turned their eyes to the future hoping it would all be over soon as Jesus came for them.

This contrast in emphasis is still with the Christian church today. Many groups anticipate the day when the kingdom will be established in heaven, and God will rescue humanity from this world. A more wholesome biblical approach would be to give thanks for God's salvation, love, and mercy in the present and then relax about the future, convinced that we and our future are secure in the hands of God. Friedmann says: "The kingdom (and not merely personal salvation) is the real concern of the reborn disciple of Christ. The kingdom may have been realized already in the small brotherhoods which sprang up everywhere, nuclei of love and sharing, where hatred and violence were absent so far as humanly possible, and where sin was fought as much as possible. But also, the kingdom is still coming in all its completeness, and the people were preparing themselves for it by full participation in those fellowships here on earth." (*The Theology of Anabaptism,* p. 110).

This call to help build the kingdom of God is a call to create communities of the redeemed here on earth right now, communities where people can discover the present joy of salvation and experience the assurance of hope for the future. It is the challenge to be a "colony of heaven" which is a living witness to the reality of God's grace and power. The church has at times been referred to as an outpost of heaven, a group of people in this world who are living under the command of a world yet to come. These people have accepted the reality of God's love and forgiveness. Since they have made the forgiveness of God a central element in their lives, they can readily forgive others, even their enemies. Because they know the love of God, they endeavor to love other people even when that is not the easiest thing to do. These communities reflect an approach to life which is based on the experience of God's presence now and the assurance that this same God is Lord of the future. Since this is the case, Christians need not fear what the future holds for their security is in Christ.

Bob Taylor

The excitement and security which Christians have, knowing that God is in control of the future, brings a freedom to live in peace now, knowing that ultimate victory has been won. Indeed, we do see through a glass darkly, for many other forces are trying to influence our behavior, but then we shall see face to face for we shall be in the very presence of God.

The Kingdom of Heaven and the Purposes of God

Matthew gives an assuring word on this issue of the kingdom of heaven. He cautions people against running around frantically trying to make sure they do not miss out when Jesus comes. There will be all kinds of people saying, "The Messiah is over here; come quickly." When that happens, Jesus advises, don't get upset. You are already in the kingdom; you are not going to be missed. Use the time which God has given you to witness to the presence of the kingdom, inviting others to live this new life of love and wholeness with you (Matt. 24:23-28).

This concept of mission is central for the believer who lives in God's kingdom. God has begun a new creation (2 Cor. 5:17), and part of that process involves restoring the old creation to new life (Rom. 8:21). The Christian church shares in that creating and restoring process, endeavoring to bring new life both to the creation itself and to all the people who share in the created world.

God's original purpose in creation was to have a world where people could live together in harmony—harmony with God, with the world, and with the people in the world. God intended that resources be used for the good of all, that food be shared so that everyone had enough to eat, that all people have clothes to wear and shelter in which to live.

Jesus told those who were caught up in possessing and consuming in great abundance that they should repent and live differently to be members of the kingdom of heaven (Matt. 19:16-24; Luke 19:1-10). Dare Christians today assume that this message of Jesus has changed?

Christians were once accused of being people who turned the world upside down (Acts 17:6) as they declared that Jesus is Lord. Looking around today, it is embarrassing to see Christians trying to keep that very thing from happening in our own society. In fact, Christians are often the leaders in frantically trying to guarantee that the world stays "right side up," even though that is often "wrong side up" from God's point of view. It is sometimes hard to remember that Christians are to be "kingdom of heaven persons" living in a society that is still committed to "kingdoms of this earth thinking." When the church drifts into "kingdoms of this earth" thinking, much of the power of their witness has been lost.

It is a natural human tendency to want to put the kingdom of God on an equal plane with the kingdoms of this earth, believing that, in such a contest, the kingdom of God would surely win out and right would once again rule in the world. But Jesus does not talk about his followers conquering the rest of the world so they can rule over the world. He does indicate that this is what the kingdoms of this earth will try to do—to conquer each other and enforce rule upon each other. Jesus said that with his followers it should be different (Luke 22:25-27); they are to be servants of others, helping all to live in peace.

The gospel of the kingdom helps to set priorities for

Christian living. Paul said in 1 Corinthians 7:30-31 that if we buy things, we should remember that we do not have them to keep forever; and if we use the world's goods, it is only temporary for this world is passing away.

The knowledge of the presence of the kingdom of heaven (the invasion of the future upon us) frees believers from a frantic need to "keep up" with the world; the knowledge of the presence of the kingdom allows believers to recognize the futility of the race which the world is trying to win. The "ever onward, ever upward" mottoes, implied in so much of this world's advertising, demand that many other people in this world be pushed "further backward, further downward." Christians are challenged to speak a word of truth to the direction of the human race. They are urged to call a halt to the mad rush toward destruction, to set a new course for wholeness, sharing, and cooperation, because Jesus has opened the future to all persons. Jesus made an interesting comparison between the path leading to destruction, which the multitudes pursue, and the path leading to life, which the few have the courage to walk. (Matt. 7:13-14).

Kingdom Living

Almost always in Scripture, discussion of the kingdom of heaven is surrounded by practical comments about daily living, such as responsible consumption, practicing love for each other, sharing with others who have need. Peter illustrates this well: "The end of all things is near. You must be self-controlled and alert, able to pray. Above everything, love one another earnestly, for love covers many sins. Open your homes to each other, without complaining. Each one, as a good manager of God's different gifts, must use for the good of others the special gift he has received from God . . . " (1 Pet. 4:7-11 paraphrased).

How do the people of God discover what the kingdom of God means in their own lives? Someone once observed that most Christians already know the answer to that question. The issue is not needing to better understand what is required, but having the courage to do what is already known. May God grant to his people courage!

Bibliography

Suggestions for further reading

Burkholder, J. R., Redekop, Calvin, eds. *Kingdom, Cross and Community.* Scottdale: Herald Press, 1976. A collection of essays and lectures on the theme of the kingdom of God.

Eller, Vernard. *King Jesus' Manual of Arms for the 'Armless.* New York: Abingdon, 1973. A delightful, easy-to-follow study of war and peace in the Bible.

_____. *The Most Revealing Book of the Bible.* Grand Rapids: Eerdmans, 1974. An interesting and exciting commentary on Revelation from the perspective of the yet-not-yet approach to the kingdom of God.

_____. *The Outward Bound.* Grand Rapids: Eerdmans, 1980. A clear statement on congregational life in the Believers' Church.

Hess, J. Daniel. *From the Other's Point of View.* Scottdale: Herald Press, 1980. A sobering collection of human experiences relating how other cultures (primarily Latin American) see and are affected by our North American wealth, power, and religion.

Kraus, C. Norman. *The Authentic Witness.* Scottdale: Herald Press, 1980. A study of the integrity of the Christian witness and method of making the gospel the foundation for our lives.

_____. *The Community of the Spirit.* Grand Rapids: Eerdmans, 1974. An exciting study of the meaning of salvation, the Church, and the presence of God.

Kraybill, Donald. *The Upside Down Kingdom.* Scottdale: Herald Press, 1978. This very creative approach to Jesus and the kingdom of God is faithful to the Scriptures and exciting in its content. It identifies areas of conflict and contrasts between the way society wants to do things and how Jesus taught his followers to live.

Ladd, George E. *The Presence of the Future.* Grand Rapids: Eerdmans, 1974. A comprehensive biblical study of the subject, presenting a number of interpretations as to the meaning of the future.

Longacre, Doris, *Living More With Less.* Scottdale: Herald Press, 1980. An exciting treatment of living, showing how people can once again recover peace with the world, God, and themselves by doing exactly what the title suggests.

McHugh, Gerald Austin. *Christian Faith and Criminal Justice.* New York: Paulist Press, 1978. A penetrating look at criminal justice and the justice system, reflecting upon the kingdom of God and possible new ways of ministry to prisoners.

Sider, Ron. *Christ and Violence.* Scottdale: Herald Press 1979. A forthright challenge to Christians to be serious in their application of the teachings of Jesus. A helpful treatment of the cross in Christian theology.

_____. *Living More Simply.* Downers Grove: Inter-Varsity Press, 1980. Studies on how to live a full life rather than a hectic life, on how to reduce the emphasis on things and the pressure of competition.

_____. *Rich Christians in an Age of Hunger.* New York: Paulist Press, 1977. A careful biblical and factual study of hunger and the Christian responsibility in mission.

Wilson, Leland. *Mission Factor.* Elgin, Illinois: The Brethren Press, 1980. A penetrating look at twelve aspects of the kingdom, including justice, peace, simplicity, service, evangelism. Originally written to aid in studying Church of the Brethren goals for the 1980s, the practical value of *Mission Factor* is far wider than for Brethren only.